WHAT EVERY TEEN SHOULD KNOW ABOUT
Money, Accumulating Wealth and Becoming A MILLIONAIRE

Kenneth Daut

What Every Teen Should Know About Money,
Accumulating Wealth and Becoming a Millionaire
© 2021 Kenneth Daut

ISBN PRINT 978-1-09837-012-1 | ISBN eBOOK 978-1-09837-013-8

Table Of Contents

INTRODUCTION i

PREFACE ix

CHAPTER 1
TURNING POINT 1

CHAPTER 2
LEARN BY EXAMPLE 24

CHAPTER 3
THE MIRACLE OF COMPOUNDING INTEREST 59

CHAPTER 4
DEBT 65

CHAPTER 5
SAVINGS 73

CHAPTER 6
WHAT IS THE DEFINITION OF RICH, WEALTHY OR MILLIONAIRE? ... 81

CHAPTER 7
OWNERSHIP/INVESTING | (EQUITY) | STOCKS 97

CHAPTER 8
BEWARE OF EEYORE: THE DOWNERS AND ENABLERS 125

CHAPTER 9
SO WHAT AND NOW WHAT 129

REFERENCES AND RECOMMENDED READING 133

INTRODUCTION

I remember it like it was yesterday.

At 13 years old I had just been picked up from my new school by my mother and grandmother. Grandma was driving her shiny black 1964 ½ six cylinder Ford Mustang that she had purchased brand new a couple years earlier and my Mom was in the passenger seat. I was in the back seat and began to sift through the couple of Racing Forms and Los Angeles Herald Examiner newspapers laying on the back seat while Mom and Grandma carried on some conversation. There was an article in the Examiner about *a self made millionaire* real estate developer/ businessman in Los Angeles that caught my eye and I began to read. Kirk Kerkorian, with no formal college education, basically 8th grade, was making millions upon millions. He had grown up in Weed Patch, California and eventually bought and sold Western Airlines and the MGM Grand Las Vegas three times.

As we came to a stop light on the corner of Manchester and Lincoln, there was a momentary silence in the car. Suddenly, I asked my Mom, "Hey Mom, how do you become a self-made millionaire?"

"I don't know. Maybe you could start by reading the Wall Street Journal every day" was her reply.

And then the revelation hit me: "My Mom, perhaps the wisest woman in the world as far as I knew at that time, had no clue". **SHE DID NOT KNOW!** After all, she was a teacher and college graduate; isn't there some kind of handbook or "Idiots Guide" that shows step by step what actions to take? And now, as I thought about it, why weren't she and Dad millionaires? And why is it I never saw a Wall Street Journal at our home let alone see either parent read one in my entire life up to that point? I was truly baffled.

Looking back on it now, grandma's silence went unnoticed by me. Had I noticed, I might have asked *her* and gotten a much different response. While my grandmother wasn't a college graduate she and grandpa had accumulated some wealth. They had come out west to California in 1945 bought a home in Westchester, a small motel in Inglewood and a couple of duplexes in L.A not far from the "BIG DONUT" (now called Randy's Donut). Grandpa went back to work doing what he really loved at Arden Dairy on Slauson. Grandma got a real estate broker's license and sold homes from Pacific Palisades down to Westchester and had just retired. She would buy a new car every 10 years and was an avid horse racing fan. (I spent many a day at Hollywood Park and Santa Anita with grandma starting from when I was a baby through grade school.)

This was so much different than my Mom and Dad's experience. While my dad was stationed in Germany during the Korean War and while I was still an infant, Mom and I lived in the "Projects" in San Pedro with lots of other military families. Later, after Dad came home, Mom and Dad seemed to move us a lot. We lived in Pico Rivera, El Monte, Lakewood, Inglewood, Hawthorne and now Westchester where they bought Grandma's house after Grandpa died. It wasn't until my mid 40's that I found out that the reason we moved so often was because they had lost the first three houses to foreclosure, according to cousin Tony Milton. More to come on that later.

This was the beginning of my journey into understanding the world of finances. I always wished I had a book like this when I was younger. I came to realize over the years that any book or study at home kit "guaranteed to make you wealthy overnight" was bogus B.S. What will make you wealthy is pure and simple: **knowledge**. Knowledge of how to grow money and make money be your employee.

"An investment in knowledge pays the best interest."
Benjamin Franklin

The one thing Grandma, who seemed to possess what is known as "street smarts" taught me was to be wary of "con artists" and *never* let someone else control your money. Having been a young adult in the 1920's she was fully aware of the original Ponzi scheme and was convinced that mutual funds in the 1960's were the same thing and to be avoided. She also learned a lot from dealing with bookies all over town, some of whom were con artists to boot. She was the wiser one and never bet more than she could afford to lose. She was cautious and would never dream of letting someone else manage her investments.

If you've picked this book up and read up to here so far, I would like to congratulate you on your curiosity on how one becomes wealthy in the USA. I assume, because of the title you are probably a teenager or perhaps older and just inquisitive. Unfortunately, there isn't exactly a single magic formula to become a millionaire. It took me until my mid 40's to cross the "millionaire" mark and my mid 60's to cross the eight figure bar. I made a lot of mistakes and I hope to show you how to avoid them as well as learn the things that **do** work to help you build wealth but especially things that will **prevent** you from gaining wealth. I am by no means a Mark Cuban or Charles Shultz. I am no tech guru, nor an inventor of some great gadget, nor a sports legend. My total inheritance from my parents was miniscule (around $7,000 if I recall, certainly not life changing). I'm just an average guy that figured out a way to wealth (albeit slow but sure) that hopes to share this information with some curious kid like I was. I may be called a self made millionaire although I owe a lot of thanks to people who helped me on my way in particular **my wife** who possessed street smarts, guts and follow thru to help us complete many projects. I can't think of enough praiseful adjectives to describe the many things she did to help make our projects successful but persistence and follow-through are definitely a couple. I may have had the dream and the courage but she had the right amount of courage and caution needed to complete projects on time and within budget. I doubt we would be where we are if it wasn't for her. I think we make a great team. She was beside me every step of the way. If I use the word "I" please know that it is really "we" in most cases. Hopefully, you can use our advice and be as financially successful and hopefully accumulate wealth even faster than we did by avoiding the pitfalls we experienced.

I can tell you one thing: My multi- million dollars isn't much compared to other millionaires and I know I am certainly not the best at creating wealth. In fact, I'm almost embarrassed that I am writing this book when there are so many people out there with hundreds of millions or even billions. I just want you, at your age, to start thinking about and working toward your goal. The point is, you don't have to be super smart "book-wise" in this country. So many less educated people have worked hard and made the right moves and become extremely wealthy self-made **BILLIONAIRES**, Kirk Kerkorian for example who never went past 8th grade. (Don't you even think about dropping out!) And on the other hand, we have met lots of "educated fools" with multiple degrees, who couldn't figure out their own finances yet had plenty of advice for others. In any case, I'm just happy to pass along what I've learned in the last fifty-four years and hope you find it useful. I hope this turns out to be the book for you that I yearned for at thirteen, that at least plants the seed of curiosity into your financial literacy education.

"He was so learned that he could name a horse in nine languages; so ignorant that he bought a cow to ride on" Benjamin Franklin.

The sad thing is that the majority of schools never teach about financial literacy or even how to balance a checkbook. My guess is that, like my mother, who was a teacher, most teachers don't know how to become financially independent, let alone comprehend some basic personal economic principles or perhaps the educational system doesn't think you need to know this stuff until you graduate from college. I had a manager once who was an immigrant from Belize who had a sign on his desk that said

"If you're so smart, why ain't you rich?" Turns out there are two types of education: The first is what you learn in school and the second is what you learn in real life from experience sometimes called "street smarts". You need both to make it big.

The majority of people however, seem to work their butts off and not "get ahead". That was also part of my question at 13. My dad had a secure job working for the State of California in what was then called the State Division of Highways (now called Caltrans) in various capacities. He took a bus from our Hawthorne, California, house to downtown Los Angeles, First and Spring Street, to and from work. He would occasionally paint houses on weekends for extra cash or sometimes went to the police auction to buy bicycles for us to refurbish and sell. He was also in the National Guard most of my childhood which required one weekend a month and two weeks in the summer. My mom taught school full time at various Catholic schools in the South Bay and in the summer she would tutor kids in a makeshift classroom my dad built in the back house we had in Hawthorne.

I once asked my dad why the neighbors always seemed to have time on the weekends to watch baseball as a family, drink beer and BBQ at home whereas we always seemed to be working. Why have we never watched baseball on TV? His reply was perhaps because of his Midwestern upbringing of hard work but it was something along the lines of 'that's for lazy people', especially the watching TV and beer drinking part. Dad pretty much only drank beer on St. Patrick's Day, 4th of July and Christmas and even then, not a lot. He refused to watch daytime TV; period.

The big question, why were we broke? Why was it "too expensive" for me to play little league when I was 6 years old? Why was it that in first grade at the end of the month my dinner sometimes was a fried egg with a hard or broken yolk. Lunch, always in a brown bag, was also a fried egg sandwich wrapped in wax paper (pre-ziplock baggie days) during the last three to four days of the month. It seemed like all the "rich" kids had lunch pails imprinted with pictures of TV shows like The Rifleman or cartoons like Mighty Mouse. They would have peanut butter and jelly sandwiches, chips, a piece of fruit, a cookie and maybe even a thermos. (Things got better in second grade and I started seeing PB&J or bologna sandwiches in the bag.) Why was it at the end of the month we were always out of money until pay-day (the state used to only pay once a month)? There was an old joke-saying, "There's too much month at the end of the money." I remember one Christmas my dad got our Christmas tree at 10pm Christmas eve. I asked why did we wait till then? He told me that was because after a certain time on Christmas Eve the tree lots gave the trees away for free. Made sense to me then but I knew something was not right and yet, I had no control over anything. Being a kid all I could do was mentally observe and compare. I must have heard "Because we cant afford it" a million times growing up. Please don't get me wrong, I was not jealous or envious of the other kids, I just sincerely couldn't understand the reason why they had and we didn't.

"There are known knowns; there are things we know we know. We also know there are known unknowns; that is to say, we know there are some things we do not know. But there are also unknown unknowns-the ones that we don't know we don't know. It is the later category that tend to be the difficult ones" Defense Secretary Donald Rumsfeld, February 2002

At thirteen, I didn't know what I didn't know about accumulating wealth. I didn't even know how to get a subscription to the Wall Street Journal let alone know how to decipher what it was saying. I was almost convinced by some, like the nuns at school, that there were two kinds of people in the world, the rich and everybody else. The rich got rich because they were highly educated and from good families (whatever that meant), but these stories of self-made millionaires with little or no education were shattering that theory. There was an old joke that God so loved the poor, that's why he made so many of them. It would be years later that it occurred to me that the nuns, who had dedicated their entire lives to their faith in Jesus and the church, had also taken a vow of poverty. What would they know about wealth accumulation? They were the wrong ones to ask.

Where was the blueprint, the game plan or step by step class on how to get wealthy? No one knew and some would politely laugh about it when I asked. Some actually said to me, "If I knew, I wouldn't be standing here talking to you". Still, why do some people succeed and others fail money-wise? I mean no 13 year old kid says, "When I grow up I want to be broke, living paycheck-to-paycheck or living off government assistance." What were the stepping stones I was looking for? What did people do *or not do* that made them poor? Didn't everyone want to have abundance and be wealthy? What I needed was some way to discover where I was and where I wasn't so I would know where to go. I wanted the simple answer to the algebraic formula that I could copy and apply to my own self.

"God doesn't want you to have just enough to get by. He wants you to have abundance!" Joel Osteen

PREFACE

The title of this book reflects what I wish I had available to me at age thirteen. The desire to develop wealth and my curiosity on how to do it became a basis for setting financial goals and working towards their fulfillment. I found that learning through my own experience as well as through the example of many successful people I either met or read about in books influenced me and the decisions I was to later make. This, to me, brings happiness; that is the gradual step by step in the right direction to attainment of one's goals. Being young, you probably won't realize till later years that your preconception of what being wealthy is, is actually not necessarily reality. Buying cars, watches, jewelry and clothes certainly does not make you become rich nor does having wealth or expensive "toys" or lunch pails make you *HAPPY*. Please don't make that mistake.

Many people have the mistaken belief that money can buy happiness. It's in all the media advertising you see for every product under the sun. People smiling, laughing, gathering with friends or family to enjoy a (*insert any product here*) which makes them all so happy. All you have to do is buy *this* product and you too will enjoy life like the *actors* in the commercial do (they are just actors in case you didn't realize).

As the late Reverend Billy Graham reminded us, "Happiness is a byproduct, a bonus that comes when we seek what is really important." He also said, "Unhappiness is like pain- it is only an effect of an underlying cause. Pain cannot be really relieved until the cause is removed."

What is the cause of hard working people being painfully poor? There has to be an explanation. How would you remove the cause?

Someone once said to me that we are all born into financial slavery and we each have to buy our own freedom. This would also be called financial independence. As long as you work for someone else, even if you're a million dollar celebrity or sports figure, you're not 100% financially independent. Felix Dennis, in *How To Get Rich*, mentions that "There are only two types of work in the world, those that change the matter on the earth and those that tell others to do so. The first type is hard work. The second type pays more. When you are financially independent you are living off your investments not off your employer's generosity. Work becomes non-compulsory." The idea is to make your money become your employee and work for you.

We are not what we call "Private jet rich" but I can assure you that we are 100% financially independent.

"Curiosity is the path to freedom itself...it is a form of power, and also a form of courage" Brian Grazer, A Curious Mind, The Secret to a Bigger Life

If you're young, you're richer than everyone older than you. What you do on the long road stretched before you is your choice. I hope this book will work to empower you to be your own economic success. Ten or twenty years from now, when you look back at these decades, will you be impressed with how you spent your time?

That being said, Ella Fitzgerald once said, "I've been rich and I've been poor and rich again and I can tell you being rich is better."

Others have said that the best part of their achieving their goal of financial independence was the unforgettable experiences, and challenges they had getting there.

And lastly, many have said that the first million was the hardest.

The first step begins with financial awareness. I hope this little book will act as your starter reference guide as to what goes on in the world of money and how to accumulate wealth albeit not "get rich quick" but rather "get rich smartly" which may be slower but surer. I hope to show you a smattering of well known "secrets" that just aren't taught in schools. Just hang in there. The younger you are when you learn about personal finances the better off you'll be later in life. Had I had a book like this at thirteen I probably would've avoided a lot of mistakes and paid more attention to my finances. Had I known what I now know I'd probably be worth a lot more than eight figures today.

"You'll never get rich by working for someone else," I was told many times as a young man, "but you gotta start somewhere".

CHAPTER 1

TURNING POINT

This first chapter is about a life changing thought pattern that really affected me. Before I can discuss that, you need to know a couple of things that led me to this place.

I was no great student in high school, got by with C's mostly. I went from ten years in Catholic school (paid by grandmother, I suspect) to public high school for my final two years in high school (mostly because of poor performance at St. Bernard's High School). My greatest challenge at Westchester High was trying to concentrate amidst a vast sea of mini-skirts after 10 years of only seeing girls in school uniforms.

Around age sixteen, I was given a flyer at school that said something about learning about becoming an entrepreneur and starting a business. This sounded like something I wanted to know about and signed up for Junior Achievement. It was not at the school but a building somewhere in Culver City, California. They took a large group of kids my age and divided us up randomly into groups of twelve or fifteen. I didn't know anybody there. Each group was led to a conference room where two volunteer businessmen explained to us that we were going to learn about starting a business, manufacturing and selling a product by actually doing it in real life. At the end of the semester we would divide up the profits, if there were any, equally among our "company" shareholders. We were to pick the name of our company, the officers of the company, the product we would create and produce, determine production costs versus the sales price, and basically everything a small company needed to do to be successful. We met weekly for an hour or so at night for our "corporate meeting" where we voted on all our product design decisions. Our product was trivets and we surprisingly sold a lot of them and made a nice profit. Each one of us got $85 when we split the profits at the end. The things we learned fostered ideas that even teenagers could successfully run a small company and what the important things were to make it happen. Knowing that there was a set deadline, the end of the semester, we had to manage our time well. I'll never forget JA and the fun we had running our company and making money for ourselves not an employer.

I worked throughout high school, first at Daily Construction News, a construction newspaper in downtown Los Angeles near 4th and Hill. I took the bus from 83rd Street and La Tijera to Pershing Square and then walked to the building I worked in. That was just for the summer between 8th and 9th grade. After that, during the school year, I got a job much closer to home working at a gas station for minimum wage filling cars with gas, washing car windows, checking oil and tire pressures. My Dad got me both of these jobs.

The gas station owner, Hal Gruskin and his wife, ran the business and made sure employees were never idle. When there were no customers he had us cleaning the bathrooms and the toilets and maybe some light maintenance like painting the base of the gas pump islands. I started at $1.25 an hour and by the time I was a senior in High school I was making $1.65, the minimum wage in California at the time. By the way, gas was $0.26 a gallon then.

I learned a number of things from him about business first of which was to be competitive. His Mobil station was at an intersection that also had a Texaco and a Union 76 (now called Unocal) station on two of the other corners. He was always the busiest of the three stations. One day I asked him why he was *always* the busiest of the three. He put one hand on my shoulder and pointed to the other two stations posted price signs and said, "look at their prices, now look at mine. I'm always cheaper. I make sure that I am always at least one to two pennies cheaper per gallon than either of those guys *no matter what*." One penny? Really? Can that really make a difference in customer volume? The real point was that neighborhood customers could always rely on him being the cheapest and that way, without hesitation, they would automatically and habitually pull into his station. But there was more.

> "A single conversation across the table with a wise man is better than ten year's mere study of books."
> Henry Wadsworth Longfellow

> "He who walks with the wise grows wise." Proverbs

Besides always having the cheapest gas on the three corners, he was a "clean freak" much like Ray Kroc, founder of McDonalds. The entire property had to be litter free and especially cigarette butt free, and believe me there were a lot to pick up back then. He had us address all customers, as we walked up to their window with "Yes sir, may I help you?" or "Yes ma'am, may I help you?" No matter how much gas they requested, we were to always wash the front and back windshields, and ask them if they would like to have their oil or tire pressure checked. If the side windows were particularly dirty we were to automatically do them too. There was to be only one of us doing all this per customer, unlike the old time film footage you occasionally see from the fifties where six guys run out to the car and did all this at one time together like a NASCAR pit crew. To sum it up, it was always clean, polite, total service, reliably at the lowest price. I guess you could say that since there was just one attendant for each customer, the service was personalized and the customers loved it. Now I realize that there was a gentle upsale of oil, wiper blades, batteries or tires just by being attentive and letting the customer know my observations of those items. "Ma'am, I noticed your engine oil is a quart low but it is also very black. When was the last time you had the oil changed?" Or "Excuse me sir, while I was filling your battery I noticed the expiration date on it has already passed." And while cleaning the windows, "Looks like your wiper blades are shot. Do you have time to replace them right now?"

I would often look across the street to the other filling stations. More often than not, they had hours and hours of no customers at all. Sometimes, they had less than a dozen cars at the end of the day. Back on my side of the street, if we only had 100 customers in a day, it was a *very* slow day.

Later, as a senior in high school, I learned that I was probably working more hours than allowed by law for my age. When I first started at Hal's, I only worked weekends during the school year and full-time (40 hours) during the summers. During my junior year I started working weekdays and weekends. During my Senior year someone at school told me that I could get class credit for working so I went to the councilor and applied. As he filled out his form, he asked me, "Ok, what hours are you working?" The stunned look on his face when I told him "4p.m. till midnight on weekdays and 6a.m.to 2p.m. on weekends, maybe longer if someone called in sick, and of course a couple days off sometime during the week." quickly turned to anger and disbelief. I really thought he was accusing me of lying when he loudly blurted out, "That's impossible!" He immediately contacted Hal by phone and told him it was illegal to work a seventeen- year old that many hours. Hal agreed, signed a paper for me to get class credit and I went back to work as usual.

I had a Passbook Savings Account at Security Pacific Bank at and in those pre-computer days you had to physically go to the bank to cash a check. A passbook was a small book with a blank ledger on each page. When you deposited or withdrew money from your account, the bank teller at the window would handwrite in the small book, how much you deposited or withdrew and initial next to each transaction. I rarely saved any money in it but the account was needed for the privilege of cashing my check there. Otherwise, without an account, I would have to go to the bank that the check was drawn on (Hal's bank) to cash it and that was a hassle.

It was almost like I felt it was my duty to spend my entire (around $76 after taxes if I recall) paycheck each week. I don't know where that idea or thought process came from. Saving a regular amount at regular intervals was unheard of to me — and probably my friends too. It certainly wasn't an idea my parents ever entertained.

Hal had accumulated three more gas stations during the 3 1/2 years I worked for him and actually had entrusted me to manage one of them in Inglewood, California. I say manage because very often I was the only employee there for the entire day. I didn't get paid any more money but I liked being alone and being trusted. He knew exactly how much money should be in the till after auditing the amount of gas and oil sold at the end of the day. Although he kept the price cheaper, like at his other stations the sales traffic for gasoline wasn't as great. It was as if the price didn't matter in this neighborhood. Rarely was there more than 2 cars getting gas at a time. So more time for clean-up or inventory...yippee! (me, being sarcastic).

It would be years later that I realized that working for Hal had taught me something called **soft skills**. These are the skills you learn by working with others. Soft skills include how to interact with others effectively including difficult customers, adapting to new environments or situations, prioritizing job duties, showing leadership when teaching new hires how to get things done efficiently, and how to solve situations when there was no manager there to take the reins.

After graduating high school, I left Hal's and took *the job* that the nuns had warned me about for the eight years when I was at St John's Elementary School. Typically, it went something like "If you don't learn your multiplication tables Kenneth, you'll end up as a ditch digger! You don't want to be a ditch digger, do you?". "Of course not Sister," and silently made the sign of the Cross. Horror of horrors, I became a "ditch digger!" My Dad had met someone who owned an electrical construction company and asked if they had any job openings. The guy said "Yeah, for a general laborer". I was 17.

My first jobsite was in Hermosa Beach, California in the summer of 1970. The job was installing a new fangled thing called "cable TV" which we put the trunk lines underground throughout the city using conduit and pulled the wires through them. Prior to that, because of the hills, the people had television antennas on poles standing 40 feet high. The foreman, Dave Smith, was a cool guy about twenty-three years old and it seemed like most of the guys on the crew were about his age. Turns out they all knew him from high school in Orange County and several were Vietnam vets, newly returned home. All I had to do was watch them and do what they did or whatever Dave said. I started at an amazing $5.17/hr. That's a 213 percent hourly increase over what I was making at the gas station. I was rich! The nuns were wrong! The Hermosa job would last more than a year. We had another cable TV job in Thousand Oaks, California, followed by a street lighting job in Newport Beach, California. After that, I worked with Doug's crew that replaced heavy gauge aluminum poles on freeway signs all over California, with wooden ones (for safety reasons). My first job on this crew was working on Interstate 15 from Barstow, California to the Nevada state line and back. My most memorable sign was ZZYZX ROAD, two on each side of Interstate 15. Everyone I know has seen the "ZZYZX ROAD NEXT RIGHT" on their way to Las Vegas.

After proudly showing her my first weekly paycheck, Mom said, "You should put some of that money away each week". Thinking she was onto something, "How much I asked?" "Try a $100 a week" and so I began with my old savings passbook account that probably had about $125 in it to start. I was taking home after taxes, more than $176 a week so I just figured, yeah why not spend the $76 a week or so that I'm used to and deposit the rest. I wouldn't even notice it.

And so it began, an accidental fall into the "Pay yourself first" method.

My job, on the Hermosa Beach, California, crew, was to follow behind the concrete saw guy, get the 60 lb jackhammer out of the air compressor storage box, break up the concrete square cut in the street, sidewalk or alley, pick up and throw the concrete pieces onto a dump truck and then dig a "pothole" where the concrete was removed about 3-4 ft deep. I didn't know the politics of what was going on in government about wages but it seemed like in a matter of a couple months we all got a raise to a little over $9 an hour.

I still lived at home, and my mom usually made my dinner. I would buy a banana and a bottle of coke for breakfast and fast food for lunch. Mom and Dad didn't charge me rent. Even though I spent a lot on my dates, I had more money than ever left over so I was able to give myself a raise for my spending cash to $100 a week and just started saving more at the bank when I cashed my check. Whatever was over $100 that week, could be 2-3 hundred dollars depending on overtime, I deposited. About a year and a half later I had over $10,000 in my little passbook account and I still didn't have a checking account yet! I was eighteen and a half and paid cash for everything.

THINKING

Mom came to me one day and said, "You've got over $10,000 saved up, you should think about buying a house. Let's go look at some open houses this weekend." I said ok and that Saturday we went and looked at two open houses in Torrance, California on Anza Street. Both houses were on the same street and were of similar design.

We toured each place, one was asking $45,000 and the other $40,000. They both seemed ok but I wasn't overly excited. My $10,000 would make a 25 percent down payment. I tried to envision myself living there. That was it and we left. When we got home Mom asked me what I wanted to do. I was hesitant and afraid to make decisions back then. So I replied, "I'm going to think about it and tell you tomorrow morning".

Note: A down payment is the amount of money you have saved up to make a large purchase. It is generally expressed as a percentage of the sale price such as 25 percent down. The remainder of the purchase price is covered by a lender making a mortgage loan. More on mortgages later.

What I was thinking all night was 1) I really loved my girlfriend and wanted to marry her, 2) Over and over again my friends on my crew and I had remarked that we had noticed there were no old men doing what we were doing, 3) My girlfriend's Dad was a successful attorney whom I highly admired and I thought that was a career I would really like to do. 4) I also recalled a family vacation in 1968 to San Clemente with my parents where we walked through town at night and saw an ad in a real estate office window for a triplex for $33,000. How could these single family houses in 1971 be worth more than a triplex just a couple years ago? 5) At nineteen years of age, owning and living in a house by myself seemed a little scary. After all the only furniture I owned was the full size bed I had bought myself a few months earlier.

In the morning, Mom asked "Well what did you decide?"

I said confidently, "I've decided to go to college and get a good job". And so the decision was made. My plan was to use my savings toward college expenses and not have to work through school. I would go to junior college for two years (very cheap) and then transfer over the class credits to a state university like UCLA for two years, graduate with a B.A. and then go to law school. My Dad made me promise not to get married until after I got my A.A. degree from West LA J.C.

"Everybody has a plan until they get punched in the face."
Mike Tyson

I had no clue what the economy or the politics was doing but let me just say in a matter of three to four years, it seemed like those same houses that

I looked at in Torrance were going for over $120,000. Inflation was a word you heard in every newscast and later there was even something called the "misery index" that was mentioned frequently. Unions were going on strike every week for higher pay and benefits. Suddenly, it seemed like whatever cash you had wasn't enough. I would need $30,000 to make a 25 percent down on those houses now if I wanted to buy. In other words, my purchasing power had gone down dramatically. Incidentally, I remember the price of gas in Los Angeles went up dramatically something like $1.50 a gallon.

By the way, when you're used to spending $100-200 dollars a week on going out on dates it's a hard habit to change. I didn't change my spending habits, like an idiot, and was out of money in less than a year. I ended up getting a job at Sears Catalog store in Westchester to pay my college expenses and I did no savings. Financially speaking, I was wiped out and I lived paycheck to paycheck even after I got married.

To save on gas mileage, I had sold both my '57 Ford Fairlane and my '58 Chevrolet Belair and bought a '64 Volkswagen Beetle. It ended up getting totaled during my sophomore year at West LA JC. My mom gave me grandma's old Mustang now, and thanks to my Dad, recently repainted Jolly Green (being color blind, Dad thought it was a beautiful shade of blue when he took it to a paint shop and selected the color).

The lesson I learned is that I could have bought one of those houses, and rented it out to make the mortgage payments while I was going to college. The sudden increase in value would have put me at $80,000 ahead. Maybe nothing would've been left over for me to pay for college at the end of each month, but I ended up having to work full time anyway to pay tuition, books and living expenses so there wouldn't have been any difference. The thing was that it never occurred to me to rent it out, I only envisioned the "living there" concept and not "the spending money to make money" idea.

"Money is only a tool. It will take you wherever you wish, but it will not replace you as the driver."
Ayn Rand

"Focus on what you can control and not on what you can't. None of us can predict the future. Your decisions are your destiny."
Tony Robbins.

I should have re-evaluated and controlled my spending habits. I could have used my savings as a tool to build wealth. My decisions caused me to lose all my financial comfort. My cash savings were destroyed.

This important milestone in my history was full of lessons that I didn't realize till much, much later.

First lesson is that with $10,000 available for down payment, I would have had a 25 percent down payment on the $40,000 house. Having good credit, a good paying job and that much cash down any bank would have jumped at giving me a $30,000 mortgage loan regardless of my age (18).

Now, some people have said, "Well you know, real estate could go down in value so there could've been a risk in losing your money."

I realize now that there are only three possibilities of what could have happened:

1. It could go up in value.

2. It could just stay at the same value.

3. It could go down in value.

So say it goes up in value, then Yahoo, Yippie! Winner, winner, chicken dinner!

If it stays the same, there are still benefits such as building up equity while your tenants help pay down the mortgage loan principal (the amount owed) and if it is a rental property (aka income property) you get to write-off depreciation of the building as well as any expenses you have on the building like insurance and any maintenance issues that cost money could be written off your income tax.

For most of my life, I was told real estate doesn't go down in value. This was proven wrong to me in 2008 when almost all property in the US went down. There are several reasons that this happened which I am not competent enough to tell you all of them, but it was like the perfect storm. Keep in mind that in my example, (30+ years before the 2008 storm) had I bought the $40,000 house with 25 percent down, my total investment would have been $10,000. That would be the most I could lose. Also, keep in mind, had I rented it out and there was a "crash" like the one in the 2008 real estate market, the tenants would still be paying the same rent, month after month and the bank payments would still be the same month after month. That means that unless I *had* to sell the place, I hadn't lost any money. Like the old adage says "Buy low and sell high" is the goal, but if it goes "low" on you, you don't lose unless you actually sell "low". So buy and hold if you can.

The second lesson was an idea that never occurred to me which was to look at properties in less desirable neighborhoods. At that time I could have bought a house for cash in a number of "iffy" neighborhoods in Southern California. "Iffy" meaning collecting rent could be challenging but with no mortgage it would be total cash flow except for taxes and insurance.

The next lesson was a more psychological type. As a clueless eighteen-year year old I had stumbled upon a method of saving some have called the "pay yourself first" method. It would be years later that someone explained to me that the goal is not to work hard all week to pay someone else (your bills) first, but to pay yourself first by building your savings. You will find that your expenses will rise to meet the available income so consider paying yourself first (saving money) the same as paying any bill. But I digress.

At age eighteen, if you can save up that amount of money in that short amount of time like I did, you feel naturally blessed with genius. This temporary success fooled me into thinking I could do no wrong. I was fooled into thinking that this modicum of success was a reflection of my "specialness". The truth was that I got this high paying job (at least it was in my eyes) due to pure luck plain and simple, thanks to my Dad and his constant habit of talking to basically total strangers. I fell into the trap of thinking I was successful and had the world on a string. I have learned a lot from my mistakes. I hope you never fool yourself to think you are an infallible Midas. It would be more than a decade later before I could say I had $10,000 in the bank again.

Two final lessons here: 1) Be kind to the people you meet on the way up, because you're going to meet them again on the way down and 2) Don't ask a colorblind person to pick your car's paint color.

Let's do the "short version" of the bad news: Working multiple jobs through college, studying like I never did before (minimum three to four hours a night), and getting a separation (and then divorced a few months after that) just as I finished my last class (an elective, Accounting 101, I didn't get it, got a D), not getting into law school (due to an incredibly low LSAT score), losing my best friend from high school, a depression that lasted years, a total loss of what to do other than move out of the apartment that my wife and I had once shared before the divorce which I now lived in alone in Van Nuys, California and back in with my parents (for six months) in Westchester. Kind of a one-two punch.Tyson might say.

The good news: graduating from UCLA (with no student debt) with a B-average, finding and making new friends (slowly), moving out of my folk's house into an apartment in Hermosa Beach, California, four buildings from the sand, meeting new friends, girls, and parties, parties, parties for the first time in my life. I was twenty-three.

Everyone on my floor of the apartment building was a guy about the same age twenty-three to twenty-five. Many of them worked at a bottled water company delivering water to homes and businesses. Some were rookie cops. None of them had a bachelor degree like I did. I had left Sears Catalog, gotten a job driving a truck for a small aircraft parts manufacturer picking up or delivering all over Los Angeles making significantly less than all of my new friends and yet I had a college degree and they didn't. It just didn't seem fair!

I think I was also partially depressed knowing that at one time, I had the world on a string and $10,000 in my bank account, two cars, and a fiancé. All I had now was the 64 ½ Mustang (painted Jolly Green) handed down to me from my Mom who got it when Grandma could no longer drive. God bless Mom and Dad and Grandma Jean.

One other thing, all my new friends had plenty of spare time after work daily and on weekends to party, go surfing or water skiing in Lake Havasu. I never did go on any trips with them because I was broke. "I can't afford it." The odd thing was that had I gotten a second job, my new friends would have probably tried to humiliate me with embarrassment. "Such a loser" so I didn't tell them about my job guarding a fireworks stand in Culver City, California, from 10pm to 8am during the 4th of July season. I had an immense fear of rejection and I expected rejection.

Mom must have picked up on the loss of self esteem, confidence and depression. One day, visiting her at her house, she said something like "Maybe you should get some business experience." She found an advertisement in the paper for a starting position at a major life insurance company in Torrance, California, which was not far from Hermosa Beach. So

I went down to check it out. I wore my high school graduation suit, a tie and interviewed.

I got the job as a life insurance salesman with a guaranteed salary of $250 a week *for 6 months* during the "training period". After that it would be a commission draw, 10% a week from my payroll bank. They would provide sales leads and all the commissions I made for the first six months as well as future commissions got deposited into my payroll bank. Life insurance was practically their only product. It is a product that's actually more of an *idea* than a product because it's not tangible; you can't see or touch a promise. Not an easy sale. Combine that with trying to overcome fear of rejection and confidence will spiral downwards.

I'll make this long painful story short: I worked my tail off for twelve to fourteen hours a day (my appointments were mostly after people had eaten dinner). Even before the initial six- month salary guarantee period was over I was definitely giving up mentally on this job. The sales leads that the manager had promised were actually a telephone book. The sales pitch I was told to use on the phone to get appointments was borderline bogus. I had lost all confidence in myself and my abilities. I felt like a total loser. And it was an odd thing but all the guys I worked with were also in the same boat. I dreaded going to work and being in the office all day with them. The big producers were *never* in the office except for monthly meetings.

"The world as we have created it is a process of our thinking. It cannot be changed without changing our thinking." Albert Einstein

Then, one day in early 1976, an incredible event occurred. I was coming up on my one year anniversary with the company when the boss announced that all the salesmen were going to go to a seminar for three days. I had just turned twenty-four. It was to be held at the Sportsman's Lodge in Studio City, out in what we in the South Bay called "*The Valley*" or "*Hell*" because of the generally higher temperatures especially in August. I didn't get excited about going except that I would be out of this office *"hell hole"*. I didn't care nor paid attention to what it was about or who the speaker was.

When I got there, all the dummies I worked with were already there and somehow, in this big room, we have first and second row seats. I am bored to death and have a bad attitude while we wait for it to start. The speaker comes out to great applause and introduces himself.

INSPIRATION

"Hello, I'm Earl Nightingale". His demeanor, his inflection and tremendous wit does catch my attention, particularly because he's not talking about the insurance business like I thought this thing was about, but he's talking about how we as humans think, and become what we think and he was looking right at me in my eyes, making eye contact over and over. He is able to mix serious psychology with humorous anecdotes.

One of the first things he says is "Whether you think you **can** or think you **can't**, you're right" and paused a couple seconds to let that sink in. He may have been quoting someone else but, damn, it struck a chord in me. He definitely had my attention. "You are what you think" and "Education is not something you do for a given number of years and stop; You've got to be learning something everyday" were among other subjects he talked about.

But the one thing I remembered most about this three day seminar was when he said that to become successful you had to 1) start with a set of clearly stated goals, 2) visualize achieving these goals 3) Write these goals down in great detail 4) Review these goals daily. There was a little more to it than that but that's the gist of it. He said you should have ten serious goals written down that you could review daily, like taped to your mirror while you shaved in the morning (it was all men in the audience), or somewhere where you couldn't avoid seeing it at least daily.

I was convinced, so I took this as a challenge and set my goals: 1) **To get a new job,** 2) To have a job that I could be proud of, 3) To have a new car (the old green goblin was an embarrassment), 4) To have a job with a big expense account. I don't remember the rest of what I wrote anymore but there were 10 things on it like he said.

Now today, I am somewhat embarrassed of the limited goals I had set but what the heck, it was a beginning. I wrote down my goals and did what he said. What is interesting to me now is that I did not have any goal in regard to accumulating wealth. I was still in the "we'll see what happens" mode of thought. I also erroneously believed that rich people were rich because they have bigger paychecks. Remember "expenses will rise to meet the available income". Rarely does a person save the money they get from a raise.

How do I implement these goals? It occurred to me that I need to create a new resume (I never really had one before anyway), and actually *apply* for some jobs on my own and *maybe* retire and replace the high school graduation suit (it was starting to get tight).

I applied for about ten jobs and got requests for interviews from five.

I did interviews for the first 4 and because I felt so desperate, I said yes to all of them when they offered a position but I delayed the start date to see what the others had to offer. Then the fifth one came along and had me interview for a job at a bank as a Business Development Officer. The title sounded impressive to me but I had no clue what it was about however, the ad did say something about "sales experience a plus".

I interviewed at their Glendale office with a guy that just didn't seem that smart but was the boss over all the business development officers of eight branches of this small bank. Instead of him interviewing *me* (because I was scared), I was determined to show no fear of rejection this time and it was as if I interviewed *him* for almost an hour basically with total confidence and the attitude of "why would I want to work for your company, what was in it for my future, what are the requirements for this job, how strong is this bank", etc. I controlled the entire conversation and had *him* talking almost the whole time. Somehow, I felt bold, confident and empowered. Towards the end of the interview *I* was running out of questions so I asked *him*, "Do you have any questions for me?" He did ask a few but not many questions.

Finally he blurted out, "I would like to offer you a position. You will receive a salary of $350 a week to start; we will give you a company car, a gas card and an *unlimited* expense account". He also mentioned that I could also use the car for any personal use!

Ding, Ding, Ding. Winner!

I never dreamed that the car on my goal list would be provided by an employer. They had me go down to the car lot and gave me a list of what was available for me to choose from. All of them were brand new. There were multiple models to choose from, most looked like small economy sedans but then THERE IT WAS! It was a brand new 1977 Ford Thunderbird. If it wasn't for the porthole windows on the side panels of the back seat, it was identical to a brand new Lincoln Continental.

I have never forgotten Earl Nightingale ever since then.

The whole purpose of this little trek into my personal history is what Earl said and I would ask you to commit it to memory:

"WHETHER YOU THINK YOU CAN OR CAN'T, YOU'RE RIGHT".

As incredible as this may seem, it's absolutely true. If you think you can never win, you won't. If you think that there must be a way and that you'll figure it out somehow, you will eventually. I had obviously lost my confidence when I screwed up the LSAT test and my divorce sent me over the top to loser land.

"Either I will find a way, or I will make one."
Philip Sidney (1554-1586), English poet.

"Believe, and succeed" Norman Vincent Peale.

When I thought that I could complete college, and actually graduate from a prestigious school like UCLA I just soldiered on through never once doubting I would complete my Bachelors degree. It was after 4 years of hard studying (three to four hours a night), my wife working as a secretary and I at Sears Catalog and multiple other part time jobs when school was out such as delivering The LA Times in Playa Del Rey at 4:30 in the morning in the green mustang, loading/unloading baggage at LAX as a Ramp Agent at National Airlines, and many more that I only lost confidence after the LSAT test debacle. That was probably the first domino to fall and my separation from my wife the second. It was downhill from there. After our split I actually lost 55 lbs in a matter of five or six weeks (I had ballooned up during college) and was now close to my high school graduation weight 170 lbs. My goals had evaporated overnight. I forever gave up becoming an attorney. I lost confidence in myself and meandered aimlessly (the *"we'll see what happens"* mode) through life. Later, I was to learn that to get back on track and develop a productive life you have to let go of the past. Dwelling on failures, reliving the past mistakes will distract you from seeing what you need to do.

"Your thoughts are the father of your deeds" said someone.

My question to you is this: One guy sees the glass half full, the other sees it half empty. Which one do you think will become a success? The deal is, your brain will "wire" itself to however you see the outcome.

Have you ever seen the reality TV show **MY 600 lb LIFE**? The thought occurred to me that these poor people weren't 600lbs all of their lives. It *just happened* gradually over a long period of years. Whatever their problems might have been, mentally they never changed their thinking pattern. Suddenly now, they realize their very life depends on changing their habits and thought patterns. On the show they see a doctor about surgical answers. He makes them lose about 100 pounds first before he'll operate. Sometimes that takes them a year or more to do that. Some never do it.

The purpose of my personal story was to show that I was seriously depressed. I was broke, my job sucked and I was going nowhere. Then, when I changed my thought pattern, with *clearly defined goals*, things began to change for me. The answer to the half glass question is: it could be either one, most likely that half full guy, but it just depends on the goals of each and their *focused positive steps* to achieve them. Don't give up on yourself because of (*insert your personal list of excuses here*). Excuses are actually little lies we tell ourselves to justify inaction. It's up to you even if the glass *really is h*alf empty. In fact, whether it's half full or empty, it's what's been handed to you. **Be grateful** you got something at all and deal with it!

"A positive attitude causes a chain reaction of positive thoughts, events and outcomes. It is a catalyst and it sparks extraordinary results." *Wade Boggs (1958 -) Professional baseball player*

There have been a million books written about positive thinking and goal setting. My favorite guy on this subject is Tony Robbins. It takes a lot more than positive thinking and envisioning to become a success. You have to have clearly stated goals, a rough idea of what you need to do to achieve them and then you also have to *act* on it.

"Faith without deeds is useless" James 2:26

With your time and energy focused you will be amazed at the opportunities that suddenly appear. Have faith in yourself and you will achieve your goals.

"Life is not all lovely thorns and singing vultures, you know."
Morticia Adams, Adams Family

If you're feeling overwhelmed at the thought of everything you've got to do to accomplish your goals and the pinnacle of your desired success seems too much or too hard, you need to try this idea. "Just for today, I will think positive. Just for twenty-four hours, I will do things that improve my mind. Just for today, I will do what I know is right. It could require effort but just for today, I'll do it. Just for today, I'll be positive". You *can* do this for twenty-four hours.

Those poor obese souls who are 600 lbs or more, kind of did the opposite. "Today is going to be just as crappy as yesterday and I have no control over that. I know that to lose weight I have to combine diet and exercise. Today's not the day I'm going to start, maybe tomorrow. What's the use anyway? It's going to take forever to get to a normal weight. I think I'll just sit here where it's safe, comfortable, easy, without challenges and eat whatever". So they tell themselves they *can't and it's hopeless.* They also concentrate on the tremendous amount of weight they have to lose to get to their goal. "OMG I've got to lose 100 lbs in order to be eligible for the surgery! That's so much, it's impossible!" instead of "Wow, I just lost 18 lbs in one month, 18 percent of my goal, only 82 lbs to go".

"A pessimist sees the difficulty in every opportunity; an optimist sees the opportunity in every difficulty."
Winston Churchill

The other thing I noticed about this show is that none of the patients seem to have a scale at home that can accommodate 600 pounds. Although they come from all over the country, it seems like they only get weighed at the doctor's office in Houston once every month or two. If the doctor has set a goal for you to lose 100 pounds by a certain date or you're not eligible for the surgery, I would think you would want to monitor your progress daily not just wait to be surprised at his office on the next visit in three months. Just getting out of bed for many of these people is a major accomplishment, but I would think they would find someone who has an industrial scale that big like the post office or a shipping company that would let them come at least once a week to see for themselves how they're coming along. After all, the goal is measurable in this case and the doctor doesn't have to be the only one recording progress. Financial goals are certainly measureable also. If you set a goal and a plan accordingly you will need to make frequent periodic checks to make sure you're on track or modify your course.

If you're still in 8ᵗʰ or 9ᵗʰ grade, you might be feeling like your goals aren't exactly identifiable at this time and so it's not *that* important to have any "carved in stone" right now.

Truth is, this is probably the best time of your life as a kid and you don't need to worry unnecessarily, but it would be a good idea to think about it occasionally and **start** getting an idea how others have accomplished their goals.

"We are not meant to remain as children". Ephesians 4:14

Ideas are beginning to evolve in your head about your future but your future success will be hampered by your lack of effort learning to read and write well as well as learning mathematics. It is very important that you realize now that your scholastic abilities will have an effect on what schools you will be able to get into as well as what jobs you will qualify for in the future. Each year in school builds upon what you learned in the previous year. My suggestion is that if you are having trouble with reading, writing or math, to look for help *now!* Be a realist and don't deny yourself the help. Ask the teacher, your parents or whoever, for tutoring help or recommending a tutor they know. It will pay off in the future. Consider that learning in school *is your job right now!* Your grades are your paycheck.

Don't forget:

"WHETHER YOU THINK YOU CAN OR CAN'T, YOU'RE RIGHT".
Your positive attitude will shape your future. Make "Positive Energy" and "positive action" part of your job description.

You will not find a class in any school entitled **How To Become A Millionaire 101.** As I previously mentioned, schools apparently don't think it's important enough to teach about balancing a checkbook let alone financial literacy or accumulating wealth. This will be an exercise in *SELF EDUCATION.* Abe Lincoln never went to college but he studied law books at home and became a lawyer. Keep reading to find out how to educate yourself on creating wealth and prosperity.

And finally, this question to you: A motivational speaker once asked, "How can you eat an elephant?"

His answer, "one bite at a time."

Failure cannot cope with persistence.

NOTE: If you have some fear or loathing about discussing money, wealth or personal finance or are beginning to have a panic attack just relax. Find a quiet place, get into a lotus position, close your eyes, take a deep breath and repeat this mantra: *"I will not be dependent on others financially when I am an adult. I will be in charge of my own personal financial affairs. I will be the boss of me."* Take a deep breath and open your eyes. Try to see yourself in your twenties or thirties. You will never get over the fear of financial education by avoiding the subject.

"The greatest thing in the world is to know how to be self-sufficient." Michel Eyquem De Montaigne, educational philosopher 1533-1592

The problem with most people in the latest generations is they open their eyes when they're thirty years old and say "What the heck?! How did this disaster happen to my personal finances? The system's fixed!" This seems to happen to people of all strata of income levels. The fabulous money they made just evaporated somehow and they don't know where it went. They don't realize that making a lot of money is not necessarily the answer. These people probably have not made any financial investments other than their 401k's or IRA's. Those expensive cars were leased, the beautiful condo's leased and the furniture rented or paid on time payments with interest. They had become what I call professional spenders, not investors. At the end of the next decade will you look back and regret the priorities you made or will you be impressed with your choices?

There are three basic parts to successful personal finance: 1) Making some money, 2) Keeping your money and 3) Growing your money. Personal finance is planning and implementing steps to achieve your financial goals. You need to learn the basic steps to managing money which means not just keeping it *but growing* it. It will take a lot of small deliberate steps and discipline to accomplish your financial goals but over time it gets easier and easier. People who forgo immediate rewards in favor of longer-term goals are more successful in wealth accumulation.

Sometimes the hardest part of the journey begins with the first step.

"It ain't about how hard you hit, it's about how hard you can *get* hit and keep moving on. That's how winning is done".
Sylvester Stallone

CHAPTER 2
LEARN BY EXAMPLE

I have a friend who owns his own insurance brokerage business who told me this story:

When he was in his mid twenties, he felt like he was going nowhere in life, his car was a pile of junk, had no money and a crap job and was becoming downhearted about making his way in the world. He felt like a worthless loser the older he got.

His father was a member of the ELKS CLUB organization and had gotten him to join also which he did out of respect to his dad but could actually care less. One day around noon, while driving past the ELKS Club, he noticed a beautiful brand new Lincoln Continental with paper plates still on it parked in the parking lot. It was absolutely gorgeous! He jumped on the brakes and squealed into the parking lot, got out of his car, slammed the door and marched right into the building. There were just a half dozen guys in the bar, so he walked in. Boldly he said in a loud voice, "I wanna know who's brand new Lincoln that is out in front!"

Everyone in the bar quit talking and turned their heads towards my friend. One of the guys said "It's mine, why, what's up?" everyone looking like something was about to happen. Like in an old western, you could have heard a pin drop.

To which my friend says "I want to know what you *do* for a living, sir, that you can afford that kind of beautiful car and be able to spend time at the Elks Club in the middle of the afternoon. Whatever it is, tell me, what do you do for a living?"

The man kind of smiled and said, "I'm an independent insurance broker, I work for myself and own my own company".

My friend told me he stood there and said, "I don't care what it is, I want to learn how to do it! I'll work for you for free if that's what it takes!" He was hired by the business owner on the spot. Today he owns his own insurance brokerage with about 10 employees.

That's what many people have described as "Fire in the belly" moment. An epiphany. A point at which people decide that enough's, enough! *We gotta get out of this place* as Eric Burdon sang in his song "We gotta get out of this place" in 1965. It is a mental change that recognizes that whatever I'm doing up to this point, **it isn't working**. We've got to make a radical change. Sure, you can sit there and say somebody back in history put you in this position and they are to blame for your current financial condition. You can sit and moan forever about how you've been wronged by these bad people in your history but what's that going to do to improve your current condition? What if everyone in the world listened to your sad story then turned to you and said, 'Yeah, you're right, such a pity"; what would that do to change your life? How would that change your attitude from negative to positive? We're all here and it's now, we've got to move on and take care of business.

"Change almost never fails because it's too early. It almost always fails because it's too late." Seth Godin

Fire in the belly is an epiphany and is probably the most energizing emotion humans have to change their circumstances. It says to you that it doesn't matter what happened before you were born, or even during your childhood, *you* are empowered to make your own decisions and forge your own future. Blaming others for your circumstances does nothing but make you weak. It does not offer new ideas, new thinking or new perspectives.

You've got to take the hand you've been dealt and figure out your own game plan. Your destiny is controlled by you and God.

I have heard it said that every living thing in this world is either growing or dying. It is also said that there are two undeniable instincts that every living creature, regardless of whether plant or animal, shares on earth: 1) The instinct to survive and 2) the instinct for procreation. In order to grow, we obviously must first survive. To live successfully each creature must continue to grow withstanding whatever adversity Mother Nature may throw at it which probably makes it stronger in the process.

Russian proverb: "The hammer shatters glass, but forges steel". In other words, some people are like glass and unpleasant circumstances breaks them (like I may have been before seeing Earl), others are like steel and it gives them incredible strength.

"Play life cool and you may freeze", Norman Vincent Peale.

"When you point a finger at someone else, you have three fingers pointing back at you", unknown. It does you no good to blame or hate other people or circumstances for your current situation. When you do that, those people and circumstances of the past are still controlling you. You must focus instead on changing yourself to make improvements. People have asked me in the past, "Why do you hate so and so?" and my answer is always the same, "I don't *hate* anyone, I just choose not to think about certain people. To hate someone, you have to intentionally think about them and I don't care to waste that kind of time or energy thinking negative thoughts."

Although there are hundreds of instances where people without degrees have made tremendous fortunes, even they would admit they were somewhat handicapped because of their lack of formal education. That is not to say they had a lack of intelligence. Many of these people had intellectual abilities and cunning that would shame most psychologists, lawyers, business advisers and accountants. They learned on the streets human behavior and business savvy and maybe a few other things they don't teach you in Harvard, Yale or other university business schools. They read books, talked to others who were successful role models and studied the market place. They took calculated risks and reaped the rewards.

The point is, don't intentionally handicap yourself by not learning to speak proper English as well as reading, writing and an understanding of mathematics and eventually at least some accounting basics and business law. The English language has been regarded as the "language of business" worldwide for over a century. Mathematics is the same worldwide and is fundamental to running a business. You need every advantage you can give yourself for a competitive edge including being sociable and communicative. You must recognize that you are in a competition against all the other thirteen-year-olds year olds in this world of globalization. Many of them are not kicking back playing video games all day, they are preparing for the big competition ahead in the game of life.

"By failing to prepare, you are preparing to fail."
Benjamin Franklin

If you were an Olympic athlete, when would you start training? One day, one week, one year before the event? Many of these athletes start training five to ten years before their event. They just don't do ten push-ups and call it a day. They are constantly pushing themselves to do more and more everyday and checking their progress constantly comparing their previous week's performance against this week's performance against other athletes performance in the same event. What's different about your event? Your event, the one that will provide for your very own future and your family? Are you just going to "wait and see what happens"? Or, are you going to leave your comfort zone and push yourself to pursue excellent achievements for results, results that will pay dividends in your future?

"The harder I practiced, the luckier I got."
Gary Player, golf legend

"Success is not the result of making money; making money is the result of success. And success is in direct proportion to our service." Earl Nightingale

LSU basketball Coach Dale Brown said "I think destiny does not just happen. It is waiting for us to *WORK* our way towards it". He also said, "The biggest mistake people can make is to be afraid to make one and perhaps the next biggest is to be afraid to admit one".

Robert T. Kiyosaki, in his book Retire Young and Rich, noted the specific differences in mental attitudes of what's important between "The Middle Class" and "The Rich":

The middle class attitudes are:

- Job Security
- A big house
- Save money
- The rich are greedy

The rich attitudes are:

- Build a business
- Apartment houses
- Invest money
- The rich are generous

He also said, "Asking for help is the first step in healing the pain of all humans."

"If you are unwilling to fail, sometimes publicly, and even cata-strophically, you stand very little chance of getting rich" Felix Dennis, How To Get Rich, publisher of Maxim Magazine.

The June 18, 2019 special issue of Forbes magazine is about the world's billionaires of 2019. It has an extensive study of the world's billionaires broken down by country and industry sector. It also shows a pie chart showing the origin of such wealth to these individuals be it inherited, inherited and growing or self-made. Australia for example shows that of the 36 billionaires it has, 5 percent inherited, 17 percent inherited and are growing and **78 percent are self-made**, the same percentage as Canada who has 45 billionaires, **78 percent are self-made**, and **69 percent of the 607 USA's are self-made** billionaires. In other words, these people didn't inherit their wealth, they did it the old fashioned way, they *earned* it. By the way, in the top 5 industry sectors for billionaires in these three countries is Real Estate, which has been my route to wealth. Just sayin'.

Here's a thought: As we all mature into adulthood and beyond, **we all become self made**. Most are not in millionaire or billionaire status but regardless, we are mostly in the status that we ourselves chose. No, we didn't purposely *choose* to be poor and target that level of financial independence versus billionaire status. What we did along the way was make what appeared to be random decisions that affected the outcome of our future. Many mistakes are made choosing the "comfortable" route. We often don't choose the road more difficult and less traveled. Instead, we often opt for the road most of our friends are traveling which appears to be the one less strenuous, most popular, fun and easy. Fifty years ago some of my cool school friends actually said things like "I'm just not into money, I don't want to be controlled by money and I just want to relax and enjoy life on my own terms", as if the pursuit of self-sustaining financial independence was a bad thing. I believe the bible says something about "you shall reap what you sow". To me, wealth is having both the money and freedom to live life on my own terms. Our minds made the decisions to take or not take the actions needed to make achievements based on what we perceived our goals were. We controlled every move on the chessboard of our lives whether we admit it or not. Certainly, adversity of some kind affected every one of us at some stage or another without exception. The difference is how we each decided to handle it and what our next move was.

The point is, a person without special talent or degrees can outperform those that do when they have specific stated goals as Earl Nightingale said. In fact, it turns out that not only did 96.5 percent of the world's super-rich not go to an Ivy League school, but 13.6 percent have no college degrees at all.

The real estate category is a broad range of activity from agents and brokers, developers, investors and builders. All involve the purchase, sale or development of land. Will Rogers, the cowboy comedian, said the best investment advice he could give was to buy real estate "because they ain't makin' any more of it". But I digress.

"Did you ever read about a frog who dreamed of bein' a king and then became one? Except for the names and a few of the changes, the story's the same one" singer/songwriter Neil Diamond,

I Am I Said

After a year at the "cool banking job", I knew I had to leave. It was not the dream job I thought it was. I came to find out the purpose of the unlimited expense account was to wine and dine existing and prospective commercial banking clients. I was hustling to see as many CEO's, company presidents and treasurers of various small and medium sized manufacturing companies across Los Angeles as I could fit into a day by visiting their place of business and or taking them out for a lunch or a dinner to try to convince them to switch all their banking business to my bank. It didn't take long for my calendar to fill up with two lunches a day and usually one and sometimes two dinners scheduled. These weren't Burger King lunches these were 'fine dining' establishments with steak, chops and fish not to mention cocktails, always the cocktails. To accomplish this, I would have to schedule one lunch for 11:00 a.m. and make sure it ended by 12:30 so I could run out to the next lunch which could be miles away crisscrossing Los Angeles, California. I remember one dinner in particular was at some famous Italian place in Hollywood, California, the client had requested and we were to meet at 7:30 p.m.. I was beat but the client had ordered scampi for both of us with cocktails and wine. As the meal progressed he started telling me his life story of sorts with his working for an organization around the world at places including Israel, Saudi, Bahrain, Yemen, Cambodia and Laos. What he wanted was a loan in order to start up his manufacturing of certain parts here that his overseas contacts needed where the final product would be assembled. Most of my clients manufactured small aircraft parts made for the big aircraft manufacturers like Boeing, Douglas, Northrop and such. They would get loans from my bank to buy drill presses, lathes, brake presses and the latest wrinkle of computer aided versions used to make production parts as long as they gave us all their banking. His loan was to be for similar types of equipment but nobody got start up loans. Loans would be scrutinized by loan officers pouring over the requestor's balance sheet and income statement as well as prior year's tax returns before making a lending determination, and, oh yeah they would have to switch all their banking business to us. But I digress.

He was an odd creature, short slender and kind of reminded me of Colonel Sanders without the bow tie but much shorter than I ever imagined the colonel would be. He had one bum shoulder he said was from a war wound decades ago. Towards the end of the meal, after much talking, he pulls out a carpet bag from under the table. How it got there, I hadn't a clue. He opens this bag and pulls out a casting, which is a molded piece of metal before it gets machined. It was a silverish color and lightweight like an aluminum aircraft part which I was used to seeing. He handed it to me and then began telling me all the manufacturing steps his company would need to do to it to take it from a casting and forging to the next stage. He then pulled out the next item in the bag, the finished product. It was about 12" long and I honestly couldn't tell what it was until he pulled additional pieces out and attached them with a slap here and a click or a twist there and finally added what looked like a small 2" funnel on the end. What he wanted was to manufacture these parts that created this device for his clients in other countries. "What is it?" I asked. It was very shiny, like nickel or chrome plated.

"It's a machine pistol. We call it the *Palace Guard*" he answered with great pride and enthusiasm. "It's basically a pocket sized Uzi" he said beaming.

I told him we don't do start-up loans and if the manufacturing company where I met him (and thought he was one of the principals, turned out he wasn't) wanted loans to purchase machinery equipment, the banks lending specialty, have them give me a call. Banks really don't like to be investors, just lenders.

On the long drive back to my house from Hollywood to basically LAX, I began to look at my life at the bank. I was eating too much, drinking way too much and really needed to re-evaluate my situation. I hadn't set any new goals since I had gotten the job and didn't know what direction I was going. The next day I asked for a week's vacation and got it. During that week I just stayed at home in a dazed and confused state as to what I really wanted to do, quit the bank or stay there. I hadn't come to any final conclusion yet when I got a call from the bank vice-president to come meet him the next day at some fancy restaurant in Marina Del Rey, California for lunch. I arrived early and waited for an hour and a half but he never showed. (This was pre cell phone days.) I found a phone at the reception desk and called his office. He said something like "Oh, yeah, uh…, uh…, I can't make it, uh… Meet me at my office at 4 p.m.."

Long story short, I got terminated. My first time ever and while I'm on a week's vacation to boot! He had some lame story about how my production wasn't up to par and I showed him a graph that illustrated my production points increasing at least 7 percent a month, every month over month without fail since I was hired. He looked startled and like a deer in the headlights when I showed him. The other BD Officers at the other branches had wild and crazy swings of up 20 percent then nothing for 3-4 months and then up 15 percent.

Anyway, he not only gave me an additional week's vacation pay but two month's severance pay. It didn't make sense but I was actually glad in a way. That was early 1978. Oh, and I had to return the car.

I learned things from the banking business, just like I had learned from Hal. I learned the things that are important when making or getting loans at banks for example. First off, they had me take an in-house class that was designed by Lincoln Savings and Loan of Chicago on how to read financial statements. It basically was everything I had studied in my elective accounting class at UCLA but it was so much more understandable and with no teacher it was self study. It took a couple weeks to complete this self-study class with tests after each section. If you didn't pass the test you had to start that section over. I passed each section 100%. It was so much more understandable than my class at UCLA but the same exact information! I amazed myself and shed the shadow of thinking I was an accounting class failure.

> "We get so used to seeing the world our way that we come to think that the world *is* the way we see it". Brian Grazer,
> A Curious Mind

The second thing was that many if not most of the successful small business owners I met had no college education to speak of and yet started up their own business' by learning on the job elsewhere. Nowhere in the lending process did grade point average or level of education get asked. It was all "nuts and bolts"-balance sheet and income statements (financials), taxes for the last three years and corporate formation or ownership documents.

The third thing was that there were recourse and non-recourse loans. Recourse loans meant the bank could repossess the equipment it lended on if the borrower defaulted and if after being sold at auction, there wasn't enough to pay off the loan balance, the bank could go after other assets the borrower might have. Non-recourse loans meant the equipment (collateral) would be all the bank could repossess. Most owners argued like crazy not to have a recourse loan on their business. The decision by the bank as to which one they would offer the owner would be based strictly on the strength of their financials using what in accounting was called the Quick Ratio. The Quick Ratio measures a company's ability to use its quick or liquid assets like cash or near cash to pay off its current liabilities immediately in an emergency. A ratio of 1:1 was the minimum to avoid a non-recourse loan. The wealthiest and most successful business owners knew their financials backwards and forwards. They could not be intimidated by loan officers scrutinizing their financials asking questions. It was like, if they had enough cash money to pay for the new equipment and didn't need the loan the bank was more than happy to lend non-recourse. Without a pile of cash in their accounts they got punished with recourse loans.

THE RISE

In November 1978 I started working at a major aircraft manufacturer in the finance department located in Hawthorne, California. I was twenty-six years old, borderline broke and desperate for a job at that point and still living with no real direction. It was a very mundane job, basically sitting in a large cubicle with six others at our desks all day long on the 3rd floor, checking long columns of figures and adding them manually on a ten key adding machine (it took a long time for me to learn this by touch). I rarely heard a human voice, mostly just the sound of the adding machines from what was probably a thousand people on this floor. I was really getting bored with this and often felt that my job was equivalent to a grocery store checker reading numbers as I pointed with my left hand and punching the ten key with my right, but I needed the security of a weekly paycheck. One day the boss called me in his office and asked if I would like to try another department within the Finance Department. I said "sure, why not". So I was sent to an area that was actually attached to the assembly line and the action and the sounds of rivet guns, drills and chatter was non-stop and deafening. I loved it and after training, began working my way up the ladder. I was required to attend a few meetings a week where my new boss conducted a presentation in front of vice-presidents and their subordinate managers. The VP's would rake the production managers over the coals criticizing their numbers and corresponding charts that I had manually prepared detailing their weekly performance. I was there in case someone was to challenge my numbers or charts and I would have to defend my calculations in front of all. It wasn't pretty if there were mistakes. I did well and gradually became well known among the foremen and managers. Later, I was offered a job with a raise in the Industrial Engineering Department and took it.

Sometime in early 1982, I did a bit of introspection and realized I was going nowhere in life and was feeling downhearted. As I began to feel sorry for myself, it suddenly came back to me what Earl Nightingale had said about setting goals. I had never established a new set of goals since that original list back in 1976 which had long been forgotten. "A specific set of clearly stated goals with as much detail for each one as possible, written down and reviewed daily". I jumped from my bed and began writing furiously every-thing I wanted to achieve from meeting the right woman to marry and raise a family to becoming financially independent. I had ten items with very specific details within a matter of minutes. Miraculously and instantly, I felt the feeling of forlornness disappear and a new feeling of confidence and brightness overwhelm me. I had my direction and believe me, my life has been better ever since.

When my wife and I got married in early 1983, our combined net worth was in the red and exceeded a negative $15,000. She had a career as a nurse at a local hospital and a six year old boy. I had established myself for five years (which meant I was "vested" a far as the retirement plan went) at the major aircraft manufacturer working in various departments ranging from finance to industrial engineering and later to facility engineering and manufacturing management. I was 30 years old and we had only known each other for four months before getting married.

Our priorities at the time were shaped by our circumstances (We've Only Just Begun, by the Carpenters now playing softly in the background). My wife was pregnant with our first child and we had a six and a half year old boy from her previous marriage. We needed the security of our weekly paychecks. Mine provided excellent insurance benefits that would cover my wife and kids, a retirement pension and a 401k savings plan. We set our goals 1) to get out of debt and 2) save money to buy a house. We made the very last monthly loan payment on the 1978 Mustang that I had purchased new five years earlier, after our first month of our marriage plus we were down to only one rent payment for all of us now. This freed up some dough to put towards accomplishing our two main goals. We also saved money by having me do any auto or household maintenance repairs and my wife was already adept at grocery store savings and coupons. (One time we actually bought $107 worth of groceries for something like $7 cash using coupons.) We basically ate at home every night and made our lunches. I worked whatever overtime was available. She actually came up with the amounts of our allowances for spending at work. I remember mine was $5 a week for a long time while most of my friends and associates spent $7-$10 per lunch. I didn't like it! After all, a can of Pepsi from the vending machine was 50 cents! At least I didn't have fried eggs or egg sandwiches, lol. Any and all extra money we got went to paying down credit card debt.

Robert Kiyosaki might have called this totally middle class thinking but we did what we thought was right and were able to measure our debt reduction and saving accomplishments with every Friday paycheck. We might not have had any cash left by the time Friday morning arrived but we were paying bills by dinnertime and the refrigerator had food and the freezer was full. It was such a rewarding feeling as we paid off each credit card, one at a time. I remember the very first credit card we paid off was a TWA (Trans World Airlines) credit card with a balance of $250, the smallest balance of all of them. I figured it was one less minimum payment we had to make and in the next month used that amount we would have paid on TWA and put it on the next credit card with the smallest balance. As each card got paid off we would put the amount we were paying on the card that was paid off and put it on the next one with the lowest balance. The formula worked and all cards were paid off in about a year.

We lived in the back half of a tired duplex on a block of duplexes in Torrance, California. Our backyard had Crenshaw Blvd. on part of it and train tracks crossing the back part of the side corner. Total lower middle class, but we were determined and unwilling to fail in our goal fulfillment. We had no doubt that we were going to succeed. We were never late on paying the rent, *ever!*

One of the first things that hit us financially was the cost of auto registration and insurance for each of our two cars both due in the same month, which set us back a bit. Annual registration had to be paid in full when due, a late payment would cost us additional money. Auto insurance could be made in monthly payments for an additional monthly fee. I felt that the extra fee was more like a penalty for not having enough money to pay in full. I decided that instead of *hoping* that we would have enough money to pay both in full next year I would plan on it ahead of time. I took the grand total cost of insurance and registration for the two cars, divided by fifty-two weeks and had the credit union automatically take that amount out of my weekly check in addition to the paltry sum I already had taken out for savings. No more waiting to see "what would happen next year". A year later, I actually smiled as I wrote the checks at the dining table. "I love it when a plan comes together", I heard the TV say as my now 7 year old watched his favorite show, "The A-Team". I was later told by someone that this was called the "planning for success method". This is just a small example of how you can have control over major expenses. Later, I basically did this for every property I owned, that is estimate what the property taxes and insurance total for the year is, divide by 12 and put it away every month till it is due. Nowadays most banks or mortgage companies will do the same thing for you by adding to your monthly payment if you request and they will put the amount into an "escrow account" till the payment is due and then make the annual or semi-annual (for taxes) payment for you. They take the responsibility for getting the checks mailed and delivered on time.

The next thing that hit us was the birth of our son in mid September. My wife quit working and stayed home until his future younger sister who came along eighteen months later, turned five years old.

During that year, I had transferred to another department with a nice raise. Someone said, "Jeez Ken, you've been in so many departments, you know all the players and what their department does, but aren't you ever satisfied? Don't you just want to stay put?" It was true and the Industrial Engineering Dept had trained me in most of the aspects of the field, at least the ones most used at this company. This time, since I liked to build stuff and now that I understood assembly factory flow, I applied and was accepted into Facility Engineering where building new factories and creating layouts for machinery and workers to build and assemble new aircraft products would be planned and implemented. It helped that I had a better understanding of assembly line flow than the rest of the group. Imagine little parts coming in one door and a complete aircraft going out the other door. Everything needs to be assembled in a logical and efficient sequence.

Apparently I did good and the boss called me into the office and asked if I would be interested in studying Engineering Management at Cal-Tech Pasadena, located in California. It would be the engineering equivalent to an MBA program and what was nice was the classes would be mostly held here at work. It was a wonderful company and a great opportunity to further my education in a work related way. Oh, by the way, the company paid 80 percent of the cost of each class up front and I paid 20%. If I successfully graduated I would have all the 20 percent I had paid out of pocket returned to me which was another incentive to complete the program which I did.

One day, maybe in 1988 or 1989, while walking through the company's different buildings, I thought I'd take a detour through my old office area where I had started ten years earlier in my first finance group with all the adding machine people. To my surprise, nearly the entire floor, an area the size of a football field, was vacant. What was once a bustling mini city of cubicles with the sounds of a thousand adding machines was gone except for a few remnant cubicle walls at the other end with wires dangling from the ceiling. I wondered where everyone had moved to. Being in Facility Engineering, I surely would've heard something about such a mass migration from one building to another even if it wasn't one of the buildings I was responsible for. I saw maybe ten to twelve people at desks with some of the cubicle remnants way over in the corner and asked them where everyone went. The answer actually stunned me. "They don't work here anymore" the guy said somewhat annoyed. "Where'd they go?" I asked. "I told you, they don't work here anymore. They've all been replaced by computers" was the gruff reply. I was stunned and began to wonder what those hundreds and hundreds of people were going through with their families and paying bills and house payments.

Later, when I was in Manufacturing Management, I learned the phrase "everyone is replaceable" no matter what position you hold at any company, maybe not by a computer or automation but possibly by a smarter or harder working co-worker or competitor. Or maybe it could be because the company thinks you are costing more dollars than you're making them if it was "outsourced". In any case, this was my first experience with the role computers would play in the future. These had been "white collar" jobs that just evaporated practically overnight due to the introduction of computers. In my previous experience at the bank, I had seen how computer- aided automation used on drill press machines had increased productivity and quality in the factory setting but never imagined office jobs being devoured enmasse. The lesson: The needs of the world can change very fast, be prepared to switch careers and have a backup plan or "side-hustle".

Working at a job is not necessarily the be-all end-all. No matter what your salary is, if you spend every last red cent on fun times, toys, shiny things and rent, you have created nothing that will pay you any income when the time comes for you to be replaced. Making big salaries does not make you "rich". What makes you financially rich is net worth. Many people have the tendency to put off saving or investing until they pay off (insert toy here: car, boat, motorcycle for example) or after they move to that bigger apartment or better neighborhood. Ask the professional sports players who went bankrupt within a couple of years of "being replaced" why they didn't save and invest. Apparently they thought that "replacement day" would never come. It's not enough to make a lot of money because in most cases your spending will rise to keep up with your income.

With the words, "You will never get rich working for somebody else" coming back to me from somewhere, I began to think and I realized that I hadn't really planned any goals past paying off our bills and buying a starter house.

We did buy that starter house. It was definitely a "fixer" (the ultimate fixer) in Long Beach, California. It was a foreclosure that looked horrible. It was so out of place compared to the other houses on the block that looked so well maintained and neatly manicured on the same street. I took three weeks off work to rehab the whole thing using all my vacation and sick leave. We even replaced the plumbing throughout the entire house, not to mention remodeling the kitchen replacing the linoleum and carpet and repainting the entire house. It was move-in ready in three weeks. We sold it for a profit three years after we bought it and used the money to help buy a very large house with a pool in Placentia, CA where we ended up staying for twenty years. Our goal was to have our kids raised in the same house from kindergarten through high school which we accomplished. This was something my wife and I didn't get to do when we were kids and so had no real roots anywhere and few lifetime friends.

The interesting thing was that from the ordeal of the first house we were unafraid of doing anything now in the new house. We removed and replaced all the kitchen cabinets, and fixtures, remodeled the bathrooms and bedrooms. It wasn't as bad as our first house to begin with but we remodeled anyway because it was certainly outdated. It was a great neighborhood.

Right about then, my work changed its shift start-time for everyone to 5 a.m. to help with the peak traffic hours on the freeways. Without traffic it took me 45 minutes to drive to work and at 4:10 a.m. in the morning there was little to no traffic. After a few years in the house and listening to hours and hours of Tony Robbins on cassette tape in my car to and from work, I began to think of and look for opportunities of making money on the side. My beliefs about not getting rich working for someone else were being reinforced and the idea of setting goals would create a future by design not by chance. I needed to find opportunities and I had a positive outlook that they were out there just waiting to be found.

"You will never win if you never begin." Helen Rowland 1875-1950 American Journalist and Humorist

I decided that I would get a real estate license not because I wanted to sell real estate on the side but because I found out that if I bought a house that was listed, I would get paid some commission (about 1.5 percent of the sale price) which could be used towards the down payment. Only problem was I would have to find a real estate broker to hang my license with. I found a young guy in the Torrance Jaycees who was my age with a broker's license. He was developing properties in Redondo and willing to be my broker. Shortly after that, my grandmother called and let me know that she was selling her house and moving to Leisure World in Seal Beach, California. She told me how much she was selling it for and I bought it using my new found 1 ½ percent and the 8 ½ percent we had saved towards a down payment. This would be our first rental property. We rented it out breaking even with the mortgage, taxes and insurance costs. I figured eventually we would raise the rent and we would have some cash flow but, in the meantime, continue to paydown the principal.

Still, with the experience gained from these first two houses I was sure money could be made by buying houses and fixing them up. I was always on the lookout for a deal and one day I saw an ad in the newspaper for a probate sale not far from our house in Placentia. I went over to check it out. It was as nice or nicer a street than the one we currently lived on I thought.

Long story short, the owner had been the original owner who bought the "Model Home Office" of the tract developer in 1965 and had died there recently. Instead of a garage door, he had requested that the developer leave the sliding glass door that had been used for the sales office in its place. It was a finished garage with carpeting that resembled an office. Everything in the house, including carpeting, paint wallpaper and appliances was original. The walls were coated with over twenty years of cigarette smoke residue. This would be the opportunity I had been looking for. I could feel it

42

deep inside me and I had confidence. After some convincing my wife gave the OK and we were off and running making an offer. The seller wouldn't budge at all on the price but I still thought there was room to make some profit so we bought it. While it was in escrow, we got into the vacant house and I created a layout with dimension details for the whole house on paper. My wife, who is a natural at decorating, started a list of what needed to be done from removing and replacing cabinets in the kitchen and bathrooms to tile countertops and floors. "The Vision" is what we called it and we could both see the finished product in our minds. Of course I created an Industrial Engineering type flow chart scheduling all the things that needed to be done in a logical order with time line estimates for each making sure the different trades weren't in each other's way or causing things to have to be done twice inadvertently.

Word to know: ESCROW, a legal concept where the asset is held by a third party while the two parties complete a transaction. The escrow company makes sure that everybody in the transaction gets paid what is coming to them in exchange for the title in the amount of time previously agreed to.

By the time escrow closed, we had a 40 foot dumpster delivered and were in there the next morning demo-ing the cabinets, removing carpets and scraping off the velvet wallpaper. We even removed and replaced everything in the showers and baths with custom tile. We easily added an atrium, due to the existing configuration of the house, with a sunken floor and French doors leading to the pool deck (with city permits). The garage carpeting was removed and its sliding glass doors were finally replaced with an actual garage door with an electric opener.

After thirty days we put the "FOR SALE BY OWNER" sign in the front yard and held an open house on the weekend. It looked like a model home. The way I remember it, it was on the second weekend of open house that a guy came in and made us a full price offer with one stipulation, that escrow must close in 11 days. When I asked him if that was enough time for him to get a loan and make arrangements for inspections etc, he told us that he was paying 'all cash' so he wouldn't be getting a bank loan and therefore wouldn't need the standard 30 day escrow. We needed to make sure the escrow and title company didn't waste any time.

Before we were finished with the sale, a local realtor came and told us what an amazing job we had done and that she had another house for us to look at in Placentia, California.

We went to the site where she gave us the grand tour room to room, and we met the current owners. I frankly didn't like the house and especially its location backing up against a major street with four lanes of traffic.

I probably said a half dozen times to the realtor and my wife that I didn't really care for it but the realtor kept pestering me to make an offer over and over and over. Finally, I was getting to the point where I wasn't sure she was going to let us leave and she said, "Just make an offer, no matter what it is." I said "Ok" in desperation and thought about it while re-walking the property and looking at the other houses on the street. My conclusion was that I will make an offer so low that she'll leave me alone finally. My "ridiculous" offer was something like sixty thousand less than they were asking and she wrote it up. That night we got the phone call, they accepted!

Although I was nervous that we were basically taking our profits from the first house and parlaying it (an old term from Racing Form days) on the second house, but that the purchase price we were paying on the second fixer really left a lot of room for improvements and profit margin. I'm beginning to feel like a house flipping genius at this point, which I know is dangerous.

Again, while we were in escrow we got in the house, made the layout, envisioned the changes we would make, called the same trades people, ordered the cabinets, tile, carpeting and scheduled the work. This time we had one additional major job, landscaping. The front yard had something like seventeen scrawny trees, all in bad shape and not attractive whatsoever, in a very limited space. They not only had to go, we would need to put in sod and an automatic sprinkler system. In one weekend, the demo was complete and trees removed. The backyard had horrible landscaping in the planter area and numerous "volunteer" pepper trees were popping up in the grass area which we had to take care of. We removed the old sliding glass door in the dining room and put in beautiful French doors with glass side panels looking out at the new landscaping.

Long story short, this house was also a model home when we were through. The FOR SALE BY OWNER sign went up when we were done, 30 days from the close of escrow when we purchased it. We held "Open House" every weekend until we got an offer after two to three months.

We made good money on both of the houses but the "For Sale" time on the second one kind of chilled the excitement. Still, paying cash, I bought my wife an almost new (600 miles on it) Mercedes 300SEL from a dealer with full new car warranty, a china set and a silverware set that we still have and use in our Hawaii house. I felt she deserved it. The funny thing is that the china and silver sets sat in a closet for decades and only came out on very special occasions maybe once a year. Now, it's our everyday stuff in the Hawaii house.

One thing that we learned early on was what customers looked at. Women looked at the kitchens and bathrooms and then the closets in the master bedroom. Men looked at the garage area, the front and backyards and they both looked at the number of bathrooms. The truth is, the wives were the decision makers no doubt about it. We determined that all future remodels and sales pitches would be focused on the decision makers. We also learned that some Asians take Feng Shui very seriously and would stand at the entrance with a compass to see which way the front door was facing. If the door was facing the wrong way, then the house would not ever be considered by them. (I'm still not sure which way is the wrong way.)

It was 1989 and I realized that the house I had purchased from Grandma was a bit far to manage. There were minor problems occasionally like the tenants frequently asking me to collect the rent in person instead of mailing a check at the last minute, and of course the occasional garbage disposer problem. Whenever they did this they would pay the rent in cash so I would be assured they weren't trying to pull anything. I did have some concerns when I came in person and I saw that the garage windows would be blacked out so I asked why. The answer was that they were doing professional photography, a plausible answer but I had my doubts.

In any case, with the "*grand success*" we had on the first two flips we made the decision to do the same thing at this house and turn it into a model home just like the first two and sell it. We had the crews scheduled, cabinets ordered, almost immediately after the tenants moved out. Everything went as planned including installing all new copper plumbing throughout the house and sod and automatic sprinklers. We even vaulted the dining room ceiling. The sign went up 30 days after we started rehab. Another model home.

We were asking $350,000 and within one hour at the first open house a man came in and asked me if I would take $300,000. I told him that this was the first hour of the very first open house and he was the first person to come in. I might consider it but I'd like to see what the rest of the day was like. He said "Ok, I'll be back" and walked out. At the end of the day, he didn't come back. Four months later we lowered the price. Six months after the first open house we decided we weren't going to reduce the price again and "give it away" since everything was so nice. So, we put it up for rent again. We ended up renting it out for ten more years. I remember my wife commenting when we finally sold it that if we had gotten a fifteen-year loan this thing would be paid off now but alas, we had gotten a thirty year loan.

The reason it took so long for the second house to sell and this house to be on the market for six months and not selling was that the economy was in a recession. We weren't *that* desperate, we could afford to hang on for those 6 months and re-rent the house because of our savings. I also decided that maybe it was time to cool it for awhile in the house flipping business until things picked up in the real estate market. We had made a substantial investment in this house that we would not recoup until we sold it. I knew it could be awhile until we could get the price we wanted and hated the idea of tenants wrecking the new appliances etc. with "normal wear and tear" but we had to stop the hemorrhaging of money somehow. Renting it out was the only answer I had.

Years later, a TV show about flipping houses in Orange County was on HGTV with Tarek and Christina. We loved the show and commented 'That was us!" every time we watched it.

We did cool our "outside job" buying houses and fixing them up for a few years. I continued working at the aircraft company and my wife was hired by a home health agency where she would do home visits all over north Orange County. Our regular jobs allowed us to be home with the kids when they got home from school.

After a few years, my wife said she had seen a business that she knew we would be good at. It was called a Residential Care Facility for the Elderly (RCFE). As a home health nurse she had visited multiple patients in numerous RCFE's. Some were very nice and some were crappy and she was convinced we could do better than all of them. It was a residential home in an ordinary neighborhood that had been remodeled to accommodate six elderly residents and a twenty-four hour staff of one or two employees. All were licensed by the State of California.

When we decided to get into this business we found the ideal house only 15 minutes away in Fullerton, California, and called our old remodeling crew to do our usual rehab only with a twist this time. We removed all tubs and created roll-in showers which would accommodate roll-in shower chairs for the staff to assist in bathing. We also eliminated any steps in or out of the house primarily for wheelchair or walker purposes. Everything was well decorated and designed for the easy access of elderly people. Carpeting was a low pile like you see in an office or bank so wheelchairs and walkers could roll easily over it.

When we opened for business after getting licensed we held our breath waiting for residents to fill the six vacancies after all it was a risk that we would be able to cover the monthly mortgage payments.

As a marketing method, Pam had "three-fold" brochures made with glossy color photos of the site and delivered them to several doctors offices that she knew specialized in elder care. With permission they allowed her to place them in the waiting room in a clear plastic stand. It was 1996 but a book by Jay Conrad called **Guerilla Marketing** written a few years before was still being talked about and making the rounds. It was about unconventional marketing. This was Pam's "Guerilla Marketing". Who would be waiting in a doctor's waiting room that specialized in the elderly? Not just the elderly patients but the decision makers, the sons and daughters of the patients who would take them to appointments (usually the daughters). As we had learned about wives earlier with flipping houses, the daughters were usually the decision makers when it came time to finding Mom a home.

Within a month, she had hired 6 employees whose shifts would cover twenty-four hours seven days a week. The entire place filled with residents, all women, many who turned out to be mothers of local doctors. Pam's nursing background had some great cache' and being relatively close to the hospital didn't hurt. All the employees were women who Pam personally trained in all aspects of caregiving from bathing and dressing to making beds and preparing meals.

One lady resident' son was the president of a major HMO health insurance company. He was especially rich. It was humorous to us that he would not allow his mother to own an HMO insurance plan (even from his own company!) but a Blue Cross/Blue Shield PPO plan instead which happened to be the same insurance company and plan the aircraft company gave me. Just sayin'.

The excellent personal service, the cleanliness and furnishings in a nice homey location made the business highly desirable. The State did monthly surprise inspections where they checked on about a hundred items on their list from water temperature in each faucet to printed menus for meals and bedding. The place consistently scored "no discrepancies" which actually means 100 percent compliant with all the rules and regulations. No other RCFE got "no discrepancies" time after time like we did.

The State inspector was very impressed and when she taught the licensee class to new prospective licensee's, she mentioned us to the class saying go see Pam's place so you can see what you need to do to be compliant. One gentleman in particular visited multiple times saying he and his wife were considering doing a business like this. He measured things, took pictures and would return frequently, usually on weekends. One Saturday, while I was there, he came by and told me his wife and he had made a decision, "That if we can't do it as good as Pam's we don't want to do it." Therefore, he continued, he had a house that they had already purchased in Anaheim, California, and wanted to know if we would be interested in purchasing for the purpose of establishing another RCFE.

We had only been in business six months in Fullerton and his house was in Anaheim, California, a location we weren't familiar with and we had some hesitancy. The house however couldn't have been designed any better for our RCFE rehab. I asked if we could lease for one year with the option to buy at the end of the lease he eagerly accepted. I called the crew.

The house was relatively new, seven to eight years old, and so renovation was going to be a bit different. We asked the Fire Marshall to come by before we started any renovation as his approval was needed for licensing. After his inspection, he told us we needed at least one more exit door in case of emergency.

Reviewing the layout, I realized that there were three rooms on one side of the building that each had a window. Outside the window was a 10 foot wide strip of dirt that ran the length of the building all the way to the backyard. That's when it occurred to us that we could call up our old French door installer to remove all three windows and put in French doors. We would call up our old cement guy and have him pour a patio covering the whole dirt section that ramped up to the doors so there were no steps giving customers their very own private patio and exit. We not only fulfilled the Fire Marshall's requirements but exceeded them and made the place more beautiful than ever.

When we were completely done and licensed we were open for business, only this time we were filled with residents in a week. The state inspector came with a film crew later and filmed our entire facility top to bottom. This film was used for training purposes for 7 years at the Orange County, California, office.

The lessons learned: 1) Find out who your customer is and who the decision makers are. Market to the decision makers. 2) Under promise and over provide. 3) Be beyond compliant with regulations and be an example to the others in your business.

Things were going great but after less than a full month in business at the second house a tragedy struck. I had an accident at work that left me permanently disabled. To make a long story short, I had two herniated discs in my neck, a concussion, three abdominal hernias, a torn meniscus tendon in my left knee and suffered from short term memory loss. By the time I had my neck and hernia surgeries I had been replaced at work. It had been almost 2 years.

In 2002 we came across another house, this time in Placentia, that would make a good RCFE. We called the old crew and remodeled to our specifications like the previous two. The place was full in no time. All of our residents were from wealthy families and paid us top dollar. We did some things that none of the other RCFE's in Orange County were doing at the time and one was that we would not only provide transportation to and from doctors appointments but escourt the resident all the way into the examination room. The reason we did this was that we discovered that in the examination room, the doctors would always begin with "So Mrs. Jones, how are you doing?" to which the resident would reply "Fine, fine, no problems". They had forgotten why they were seeing him or the purpose of the visit. The caregiver, as our employees were called, would be able to answer with whatever was really going on like sleep patterns, bladder or bowel problems etc. Personalized service, as old Hal Gruskin would have said.

We had a great reputation and Pam had become the CEO of a major non-profit Home for elderly women.

In 2006, while picking up some things at the local grocery store on a Friday afternoon at about 4:30 p.m., I got a call on my cell phone. It was a realtor who wanted to know if we were interested in selling the Anaheim facility. The timing was funny because just the night before at the kitchen table Pam asked me what we thought our properties were worth. We had come up with a number for each place based on the residential home comps in the area. So when this realtor called and asked I really thought it was just a crank trying to score some listings. I gruffly said "If it was for sale, it would be pricey"

"What would you ask for it?" she queried. I thought about the number Pam and I had just discussed the previous night and added $200 thousand to it just to be rid of her call.

"I'll call you back in five minutes," she said. "Yeah sure" I replied, never thinking I would ever hear from her again. While I stood in the checkout line, she called back and I answered. "Can we sign the papers tonight?" she asked. Unbelieving, I asked "So you have a buyer?" "Yes", she replied.

"Holy smokes," I said breathlessly on the phone to Pam. "I think I just sold Anaheim!"

We called Larry Emery, our **taxman** and asked what ramifications selling this, at what we thought was an exorbitant price, would have on our taxes.

"You're gonna get killed on taxes" Larry said, "Unless you do an IRS Rule 1031 exchange". In other words we would have to purchase another "like kind" of property which in this case could be basically any kind of property that was a rental.

Lucky for me that I had recently finished Dolf de Roos book REAL ESTATE RICHES where he clearly outlined a list of the benefits of owning commercial property and about triple net leases.

"So what do I have to do in a 1031 Exchange?" I asked? He explained that how it worked was in addition to having a third party escrow company we needed a third party *accommodator*. What happens is when escrow closes and they print out your check, you can't ever touch it. Instead it goes directly to the accommodator who holds it another escrow account until you find a replacement property to buy. This check will then be used as the down payment. The replacement property has to be "like kind" property in other words a rental property for a rental property. It could be an apartment building, *a commercial* property or even a farm that we would rent out. One stipulation was that it had to cost more than the property that was sold. We never took a paycheck from the business' and had set up the homes as S Corporations. Having read about Ray Kroc, founder of McDonalds in the book "Grinding it Out", we knew we were actually in the real estate business from the beginning and the RCFE's were merely renting property from Pam and I. So we needed to buy a big rental property to replace rental property. Most realtors we knew only did residential properties. One realtor was finally recommended who specialized in commercial properties.

She explained to us that the best deals at that time would not be found in California. She found us a eight-tenant shopping center in Jackson, Tennessee that would give us positive cash flow with a 7 percent cap rate. It was actually attached to a Target store and next to a Kroger. We bought it. More than one person told us we were nuts and didn't know what we were getting into. We hired a management company to collect the rents, pay bills and best of all figure out how much each tenant owed us based on square footage, their share of the taxes, insurance and maintenance- hence "TRIPLE NET LEASES".

We still had the Fullerton and Placentia homes and things seemed to be going well for us. Almost a year to the day that I got that phone call in the grocery store, I found myself back in the same store on a Friday about 4:30p.m. and my cell phone rang. It was the same realtor. This time she asked if I would be interested in selling the Placentia, California, home. "If I did, it would be pricey" I replied just like I said the year before. "Well what's pricey?" she asked. Again, having recently talked to Pam about our estimated values just recently, I added $350,000 and told her. "I'll call you back in five minutes" she said just like before and again , just like the previous year she called back while I was still standing in the checkout line. "When are you available to sign?" she asked.

This time my answer was different. I told her that we have two RCFE's and if we were to sell one we would want to sell the other also. So I asked her if the buyer would be willing to buy both and she said she would get back to me. She did ask how much for the Fullerton home and I naturally added $250,000 to that one. The next day she called and said we had a deal. I called Larry the taxman and found a new commercial realtor. This time the commercial property she found was in Texas near Corpus Christi. That was 2007. We had a lot going on and didn't close the deal right away.

Pam and her girlfriend had fallen in love with the Palm Springs, California, area. Pam insisted I find her a vacation home for us. The whole valley was humming with developers and contractors. New developments were everywhere. We began driving the hour and a half out there every weekend looking for the right place. We found a development that was partially built and picked out a lot with a 3 bedroom home to be built in the next couple months that overlooked the third fairway at Indian Springs. We added some personal touches such as a below ground Jacuzzi in the backyard and surround sound wiring in the living room.

Later, we met a hot-shot realtor later who convinced us that we needed to sell or rent out the Indian Springs place and move on to more desirable property. First she took us to Mountain View Country Club where an owner was selling his place that he had never moved into. We put an offer on it $25,000 less than he was asking. Next she took us to a new development called Sun City, that was still bare dirt and they were putting in the sewer lines and such. They were having a lottery for the purchase of the first 9 homes. We each put our names in the lottery. Next, she took us to a development that was underway in Coachella where we actually put in an offer for two houses that we thought would make great rentals.

Long story short, our offer in Mountain View was accepted as well as the offer in Coachella, California, for the two houses. A couple days later we got a phone call from Sun City, Pam had gotten one of the lottery houses.

We loved the Mountain View house and closed the deal. We made plans for a pool and Jacuzzi, fire pit and BBQ and landscaping. The two houses in Coachella, California, were to become rental properties. When the Sun City house was completed we put it up for sale. I made one house payment on it before selling it for $250,000 more than we paid for it. The market was crazy hot!

A banker friend of ours in San Luis Obispo told us about a great deal he found in Cambria, California. Apparently in Cambria, California, you cannot build a house on an empty lot unless it has a water meter. The waiting list time for water meters was something like two years and this lot had just gotten one. The builder had plans and permits ready to go and just needed a buyer like me to get started. So we bought it, got a construction loan from the bank and went to work. The finished product was expected to be worth over a million dollars.

Meanwhile as we glided through 2007 there was an article every single day in the paper or on the news channels about whether or not we were in a real estate bubble. We owned eleven houses at the time. It was interesting at first but was now becoming annoying. After a couple months of this daily deluge I said to Pam, "If there is or isn't a real estate bubble, these TV news guys are going to create one! We need to sell off our holdings starting with the Cambria, California, property." The contractor had called earlier that day to say he expected to be finished in ninety days. From experience I knew that I needed to find the best hot-shot realtor in Cambria, California. After a week of research I narrowed it down to two in the city and just picked one to list the property. I explained my goal to sell as soon as possible and although it wasn't completed yet I wanted it to be shown. She explained that a house like this could not actually be sold until the utilities were turned on but she could find us a buyer in the meantime. The day the utilities got turned on we closed escrow and sold it. I think we made $150,000-$200,000 on it. We got to see it one time before we said goodbye forever. It was a beautiful two-story house with a balcony that you could look through the pines and see the ocean waves white water.

We put Indian Springs up for sale after having been a rental for over a year and it sold quickly.

We also bought a two story house in Coachella and paid top dollar for it, grrrr.

We sold our old house in Placentia for top dollar and did well there selling at the top of the market. Things were moving fast.

We bought a house in Hawaii and put $65,000 down. Countrywide Mortgage had done several loans for us and said they would do this one too. I would be "a piece of cake". Time in escrow ticked by and I kept getting the run around with them losing my loan applications and passing me from one office to another, etc. Turned out at almost the last minute, they weren't going to do the loan and the seller in Hawaii was licking his chops thinking he was going to keep our deposit money. At the last minute I came in with all cash to the escrow company and completed the sale. We bought at the top of the market.Grrr

Meanwhile, the commercial property seller in Texas was getting antsy. The lender had finally come through but was requiring a major change- due to the jittery market they had to change the terms of the loan. The amount I needed to put down now was an additional $350,000. I didn't want to but rather than forfeit and lose the $60,000 initial deposit and screw up the 1031 exchange (we were running out of time) I put a $350,000 second on the Mountain View Country Club home and sent them the money.

In 2008 the housing market was collapsing and Countrywide Mortgages was nowhere to be found. Small banks like the one that helped us in San Luis Obispo, California, were closed by the government for what sounded to me like very vague reasons and yet big banks on Wall Street were getting handouts from the government for very vague reasons. You heard the phrase "too big to fail" a lot.

Another house we had bought in Coachella, California, had a lovely tenant and his family living there. He worked for a company that steam cleaned carpets in major hotels from San Diego to Los Angeles. He called one day apologizing profusely that he and his family just couldn't afford to stay in the house any longer and were going to have to move to an apartment building in Indio, California. They would be out by Friday except for the washer and dryer. His son and his son's friends would be by on Saturday to pick up the washer and dryer. He was having the utilities turned off on Friday. Because the heat out here in the desert is unforgiving, more than a couple days without water will kill a lawn quickly so I arranged to have the water turned back on Monday.

Monday afternoon about 4 p.m. a stranger called our house and introduced himself as our neighbor. He said water was pouring out of our front door sill. Turned out that when the boys picked up the washer and dryer, they disconnected the hoses to the washer. The water was turned off so nothing came out. When the water company turned it back on, the valves were in the open position and so the water came blasting out so hard it hit the wall on the opposite side of the washroom. By the time I got there, the wall had totally dissolved exposing the studs and the house had close to two inches of water everywhere. Luckily, we were covered insurance wise. The house was completely repainted, new carpeting and linoleum, new baseboards and ended up looking like the model home it once was. I said to Pam, "This is the best this house is going to look. Lets sell" and so we did and even in a down market and made $25,000 on the deal. Whew!

Shortly after that housing prices dropped like a rock. People were dumping their property left and right. One thing we were reminded that we actually already knew was that in a financial crisis the first thing people dump is vacation property. Great deals are available to those that have cash then. "Cash is King" Pam's favorite saying.

The Chinese symbol for crisis is made of two words: danger and opportunity. Our Hawaii house for example went from $650,000 to $750,000 in the first 12 months and then to $350,000 almost overnight. It has taken ten years for it to recover to the original $650,000 value.

We still own two houses in Coachella, California that we rent out, the Hawaii house that we refuse to rent out, we sold the Mountain View Country Club house and bought a condo near the clubhouse with outstanding views, the Texas property, a standalone Dollar Tree store in Tennessee and a self storage facility in Ohio. The first commercial property we bought, the eight-unit shopping center in Jackson, Tennessee, got bought out by Kroger stores in 2015. Altogether the action has calmed down but for awhile there I was worried about keeping up with the fast and furious changes.

CHAPTER 3

THE MIRACLE OF COMPOUNDING INTEREST

The most amazing thing in investing is called "compound interest". I didn't know about this until my twenties. To illustrate, most teachers will begin with a couple simple ideas.

First let's calculate how to get a million dollars with no compounding involved. If you can get one million people to send you a dollar, you'd have a million dollars right? Or, 10 million people to send you ten cents would be the same thing, or 100 million people to send you 1 cent. There you have it, the secret's out. Instant millionaire.

Unfortunately, trying to do that isn't that easy so let's try the next idea, compounding:

If you started with a penny and could invest it so that you doubled your money every day, what would you have at the end of thirty days? Tell you what; I'll do the math for you below:

DAY #	$ AMOUNT INVESTED	DOUBLED $ BALANCE	
1	.01	.02	
2	.02	.04	
3	.04	.08	
4	.08	0.16	
5	0.16	0.32	

DAY #	$ AMOUNT INVESTED	DOUBLED $ BALANCE	
6	0.32	0.64	
7	0.64	1.28	
8	1.28	2.56	
9	2.56	5.12	
10	5.12	10.24	
11	10.24	20.48	
12	20.48	40.96	
13	40.96	81.92	
14	81.92	163.84	
15	163.84	327.68	
16	327.68	655.36	
17	655.36	1310.72	
18	1310.72	2621.44	
19	2621.44	5242.88	
20	5242.88	10485.76	
21	10485.76	20971.52	
22	20971.52	41943.04	
23	41943.04	83886.08	
24	83886.08	167772.16	
25	167772.16	335544.32	

DAY #	$ AMOUNT INVESTED	DOUBLED $ BALANCE	
26	335544.32	671088.64	
27	671088.64	1342177.28	
28	1342177.28	2684354.56	
29	2684354.56	$5,368,709.12	
30	$5,368,709.12		

Wow, from 1 penny to $5.3 million in 30 days! Well that's the basis for understanding compounding. Of course doubling your money like that would be a 100 percent interest increase daily! That's not easy to do daily. That *would* be magic!

"What is interest?" you ask. Interest is a percentage on the money made or the money paid as in the case of borrowing money.

By the way, there is a simple formula that will help you find out how long it will take to double your money. It's called the Rule of 72. You take the number 72 and divide it by the interest rate. For example, if you were getting 10% annual interest you would divide 72 by 10. Answer: 7.2 years till you doubled up.

Now let's get real and look at the three major elements 1) TIME and 2) INTEREST RATE. The third element MONEY is not as important as the first two as you will see in this hypothetical example:

Say we have three people Eeny, Meeney and Miney -- all the same age.

Eeny gets a good job at age twenty-five and puts $1,000 in her savings investment vehicle that earns 7 percent interest a year. Eeny puts this

61

money in this account every month without fail for 10 years and stops putting in at that point (age thirty-five) and just lets it stay there till age 65. (That's $1000 x 12mo's x 10 years = $120,000 total invested)

Meeney starts the same exact savings plan and deposits the same amount, $1000 a month, that earns the same rate of interest 7 percent only she starts at age thirty-five. She also stops 10 years later (at age 45) and also lets it sit there till age 65. (Same total amount of investment as Eeny, $120,000)

Miney starts the same exact savings plan, same dollar amount and same interest rate, only she starts at age forty-five. Miney stops the savings plan 10 years later (age 55) and lets it sit there till age 65. (Same amount of investment as Eeny and Meeny, $120,000).

At age 65, what do you expect the totals to be? They each had the same plan, invested the same amount of money for the same number of years (ten), got the same interest rate and yet the results are dramatically different.

Eeny ends up with $1,444,969

Meeney ends up with $734,549

Miney ends up with $373,407

What happened? Remember I said the two most important things were time and interest rate? The amount of money deposited and the number of years invested (10 years) was identical <u>but the difference was the age that they **started** saving and that they let the magic of compounding do its work over the years until they were 65</u>. Eeny started ten years before Meeny and twenty years before Miney. This is the time I'm talking about.

> "Time can be an ally or an enemy. What it becomes depends entirely upon you, your goals, and your determination to use every minute." Zig Ziglar

Negative people may be feeling downhearted about their current situation and say the best time to start saving or investing was twenty years ago but a positive thinker will realize that the second best time to invest starts today.

Realistically, this was for illustration purposes only. To get a 7percent return on your money these days might require owning some commercial real estate or something but it is possible. Remember this: The higher the risk the higher the reward should be. When you're just starting to save you will need a safe investment like a savings account or a money market account. They are the ultimate in safety because each account is insured by the government but the interest rate (the reward) is low. Reward should be commensurate with risk. Don't put all your eggs in one basket.

Ben Franklin said compounding interest is the 8th wonder of the world because "money makes money and the money that money makes, makes more money". You need to start saving money as soon as possible in some kind of account that earns money, on money. Richard Russell, stock guru and investment writer in his article Rich Man Poor Man the Power of Compounding, wrote that compounding was the "royal road to riches". Please note that compounding doesn't necessarily mean a savings account, it could be in your IRA or in your 401k or dividend paying stocks. The point is that you are delaying gratification by putting it away and letting itself grow.

Compounding, in fact, is a key part of a lot of different types of retirement investments like 401K's, 403B's, IRA's, Roth IRA's etc. For example, you automatically add money to your retirement pile with a deduction deposit from each paycheck and just let it accumulate in one of a million different mutual funds or other investment vehicles. Additionally, many employers will match the amount you contribute to a 401K up to a certain amount adding more to your pile. Whether the stock market goes up or down could affect the total amount you have at any given moment if it's invested in stocks. Bond markets go up and down as well as every conceivable investment including gold and silver. (Read about dollar cost averaging.) For most of my life "experts" said that real estate never goes down, but they were sure wrong in 2008 because of so many bad loans that went belly up and market values went down.

> "It does not matter how slowly you go as long as you do not stop." Confucius (551 BC – 479 BC)

My point is, it's better to start learning about financial literacy at your young age than wait till you're in your thirties and have a mess on your hands.

CHAPTER 4

DEBT

My parents were always broke. I loved my parents. They had jobs and made ok money but were always broke, especially the last three days of the month just before payday until the mid 1960's. This is sometimes jokingly referred to as, "Too much month at the end of the money." It would be after I became a senior in high school for me to find out why but when I did it was almost electrifying. My folks were in debt because of credit card debt. It's my understanding that credit cards came out in the mid-to-late-fifties when my folks were in their mid twenties. Kind of weird, but I remember my dad's twenty-sixth birthday in our crappy apartment off La Cienega in Inglewood. My mom made a cake and both of us sang "Happy Birthday" to my Dad. We were maxed out in credit. Sears, JCPenney's, and other stores had cards as well as Bank of America. It was all based on "Revolving Credit". This means that once you were approved you could buy *stuff* using the card. They would send you a monthly statement of how much you owed but you didn't have to pay it all back, just the monthly minimum *and* you could continue purchasing *stuff* all the time till you hit your credit limit. I remember quite well while working at Sears in the early seventies and explaining to customers that they would only be charged 1.5 percent interest monthly, or 18 percent (APR) a year, on the outstanding balance which would be added to the next month's statement thereby "Revolving".

We were **piss poor** in 1957, but of course a kid like me at five years old wouldn't know that. I don't think any child cares if their parents are rich or poor as long as they are in a loving environment and have food, clothing and shelter and feel safe. Everyone in the apartment complex was in the same boat. All the dads had jobs and were gone all day. They came home, their wives made dinner; they watched Walter Cronkite on *You Are There*,

Victory At Sea or *THE MILLIONAIRE* and went to bed. Next morning, they all got up and started all over again. Maybe the moms watched *Queen For A Day* or *As the World Turns* in the afternoons if they didn't work outside the home. This was normal for us. My mom worked as a teacher full time.

In any case, I digress. Remember the magic of compounding interest we just discussed in the last chapter? What if that were in reverse? Suppose instead of depositing a $100 a month, you borrowed or charged $100 on a credit card. Now the shoe is on the other foot. You've got to pay the $100 back or at least the minimum amount due *plus interest* charged on the previous month's ending balance back to the bank or department store. The minimum is a small portion of what you borrowed (the principal) like maybe $20 of the $100. So next month your statement will show a balance of $80 *plus interest*. *But wait there's more!* Let's say you charged *more* money on the credit card before the next month's statement comes. Maybe you decided to charge $25 on pizza to watch Monday Night Football at home with your friends. Now you're $5 deeper in the hole because although you paid back $20 you also re-borrowed $25. Your next monthly statement will reflect previous balance ($80) and new charges ($25) and you will be right back where you were last month only $5 worse *plus interest* (let's say $1.20) for the $80 balance for a total of $106.20. Let's say you pay the minimum again on this statement $20 and you have another pizza night ($25) before the next statement comes. Here we go again (revolving). The new statement says previous balance $106.20, payments $20, new charges $25 *plus interest* $1.59 for a grand total of $112.79. Whatever amount you pay (less than the full amount owed), the interest gets paid first and the remainder goes toward the principal. Remember what Ben Franklin said about compounding: money making money that makes money? Look out! This revolving merry-go-round is picking up steam and not slowing down. It's money costing money that costs more money. Keep in mind that whatever payment amount you send in, the monthly interest gets paid first. Whatever is left over after that goes to the principal amount owed.

For years credit card bills would show the minimum amount due on each payment. Of course you could always pay back more than the minimum which would go towards the principal owed. But, if you were to just pay the minimum owed you really weren't making headway as you can see. Nowadays, the monthly statements not only will show the minimum due but also how long it will take to pay off the credit card if all you did was pay the minimum due on the *current* balance.

Let's say your Bank of America card bill has a balance of $234.51. The minimum due is $25. The statement shows you that if you only paid the minimum every month it would take 11 months (**IF YOU DIDN'T CHARGE ANYMORE**) to pay it off and end up paying a grand total of $250.00. This is because every month they charge you 17.24% APR (Annual Percentage Rate) interest on the unpaid balance for purchases and balance transfers. (I got this from my BankAmericard bill) Direct deposit and check cash advances are charged at higher rates 20.24% and Bank Cash Advances are charged 27.24% *on the unpaid balance.*

Now think about this for a second: $250.00 - $234.51 (original balance) is $15.49 total interest you'll pay in 11 months. That's dumb but not too horrible. *But wait, there's more!* If you continue to charge an additional $25 a month, and only make minimum payments, the balance will never be paid off thanks to *"plus interest"* and your spending habits. Oh, and I forgot to mention, if you do not pay the minimum by the due date required you may have to pay an additional late fee of $38.00 for every month you're late and as additional punishment, your APRs may be increased up to the penalty APR of 29.99%! That $38.00 is added onto your previous balance for the next statement. You could basically end up paying this minimum payment on this bill and that pizza for the rest of your life! Do you see how credit card debt is like being hooked on crack? It's a struggle to get off it but it's a better life when you do.

The problem I see is when kids graduate from high school and go off to college they will find credit card companies setting up booths in the quad taking applications and maybe giving away some kind of *free* gift just for applying for a credit card. These kids, most likely, have never seen a book like you're now reading, and blindly sign up. Unfortunately, they don't really consider **the part about paying the credit card company back**. They go out and spend on books and other supplies which are good expenses but soon find that they can also buy football tickets, nights out, Spring break, pizza and the list goes on. Suddenly they have debt that they can't afford to pay off let alone make the minimum payments. Remember my example of the 600 lb people? Debt creeps up on you similarly while you didn't pay attention.

What happens when you miss payments? As I mentioned above, late fees get attached, interest rate changes for the worse and more misery begins. **But wait, there's even more!**

I haven't mentioned yet about **FICO credit scores**. When you don't make payments in a timely manner your credit score gets dinged on your credit report. If your credit score drops below a certain threshold score, you will find out the consequences when you go to buy or lease a car for example or when you apply for a mortgage to buy a house. The lenders look at your FICO score and determine how risky you are (a risky loan evidenced by a low credit score) and what kind of *character* you have. Risky loans get charged higher interest rates (remember the risk/reward statement in chapter 3 and if bad enough are even denied getting the loan. Higher interest rates cost you more money. Also, many landlords run your credit scores to see if you're a good risk as a renter. Who wants to rent their property to someone who has a history of not paying bills in a timely manner? Your entire borrowing history will be noted in your credit report.

Now please don't misunderstand, not all debt is bad. Nobody I know buys a commercial property for cash. There's a thing called leverage, there's capitalization (CAP) rates, there's return on investment (ROI), net operating income (NOI), these are things you and the lender will consider when borrowing besides your personal credit score (which by the way is also affected by how much money you owe to other creditors) and how much you have saved up to put down. The point to remember is if you borrow money to make money, that's a good thing and you can become wealthy. If you borrow money for stupid things like toys and pizza and don't pay off the bill entirely at the end of the month, that's a bad thing and are destined to be poor.

To put it in simpler terms, think of your "NET WORTH" as your boat and every dollar in interest debt as a termite attacking your boat, eating it one tiny little bite at a time.

What you should know about FICO

FICO was originally Fair, Isaac and Company founded by Bill Fair and Earl Isaac in 1956 as a data analytics company. Lenders purchase FICO scores to make decisions on consumer's creditworthiness (risk). FICO scores are based on credit reports and range from 300 (lowest) to 800 (highest). FICO scores are used by lenders to make decisions on nearly all loans from mortgages to auto loans and leases as well as by landlords trying to decide which tenants are low risks and also by some employers to see what kind of *character* the applicant is. In fact, in Hawaii it's not unusual to find property managers not only checking Credit Score but Employment Records, Previous Landlord References, and State of Hawaii Court Records to get an idea about your *character*.

Your FICO score is based on:

- **35% payment history and reliability,** (your history of paying on time)

- 30% on amounts owed

- 15% length of credit history,(how long have you had credit)

- 10% new credit-old accounts show reliability

- 10% types of credit, ie. credit card, car loans, signature loans, mortgages you have had

Some credit cards offer airline miles or hotel points if you use their card. They will award you points solely based on the purchases made that month. They do that regardless of whether you pay off the card entirely at the end of the month or not. I use a credit card for almost all my expenses these days and rarely use cash. Why, you ask? Because I can keep track of all my expenses easier, get hotel points or airline miles for everything I buy and don't need to carry around a lot of cash. I pay off my credit card bill **entirely** each month. I've had a few bills exceeding my $50,000 limit but I pay them off when the statement comes or sometimes even before. I get a lot of hotel points, so many that I'm considered "Ambassador Class" for my hotel card which means I am entitled to a few extra perks. Whoo Hoo! (*I'm being sarcastic*). Thanks to my wife, who knows how to maximize the airline miles, we have flown non-stop round trip to London multiple times and to Sydney Australia, first class using air miles basically for the cost of taxes. This year she got us a non-stop flight from Los Angeles to Paris First Class using points. The point is though; I do not pay *any* credit card interest because I pay my bill off each month. In other words, it costs me nothing to use my credit card **EVER!** It's like I have a short term loan for no interest. There is one exception; they charge me an annual membership fee which I gripe about and have occasionally gotten out of having to pay.

I think the trick to managing credit cards is to primarily only use one or two cards consistently. It's easier to keep track of that way. I remember times in the seventies where people had ten or twelve cards in their wallets (I was one); totally unnecessary. I may have multiple cards, but I only carry two main ones.

High Interest Debt, specifically credit card debt is the most horrible thing imagined. Many cards charge over 20 percent on the unpaid balance but I think the average is 18 percent. That's what is called HIGH-INTEREST-RATE DEBT. Some car loans and student loans also have high interest rates. When you compare that to buying a house and getting a mortgage at 3-5 percent for hundreds of thousands of dollars in borrowing and yet you're getting nailed forever on that stupid pizza from three years ago on your credit card for 18-20 percent. (If you never paid off your credit card in full, you're still paying on that pizza.) Stay out of credit card debt! Do not carry a balance!

Other countries are not so accepting of debt like Americans are. In Belgium for example, if you are ninety days behind in paying off your credit card, auto or housing loan, your name is reported by the bank which triggers a series of services consisting of mandatory classes on how to budget and a psychological analysis of any personal problems that you might have that contributed to this situation such as alcohol or marriage problems. In France, credit cards are tied directly to bank accounts.

Pay off that credit card debt! Let's say you owe $20,000 on a typical credit card paying 20% interest. Do you realize you are paying $4,000 a year in interest? How would you like a $4000 a year raise? Pay off the debt! Put that extra money in the bank and hold it there until you see an investment opportunity. Now that's electrifying!

Having less credit card debt and having a history of paying in a timely manner also boosts your credit score getting better loan deals in the future.

I almost omitted something: My Business Law 101 teacher at West LA JC had us commit to memory and repeated aloud multiple times in class: "Don't ever co-sign for someone else's loan, **not even for your sainted mother!**" If *your* lender requires *you* to get a co-signer you should probably forget about getting a loan and work on improving your credit rating. Never be a co-signer for someone else! I guarantee you will regret your relationship with whomever you co-sign for. It has nothing to do with friendship, **its business**. If your buddy quits paying on his loan, the lender is going to be knocking on *your* door and dinging *your* credit till he gets paid off because co-signing means you're guaranteeing his loan, that you'll pay if he doesn't.

Financial literacy is more than just knowing your credit score. It's managing your own personal finances by making well informed money management and investment decisions. Be the boss of you. There are types of debt that can be beneficial to your financial growth. More on that later.

The next important component is savings.

CHAPTER 5

SAVINGS

Unless you were born rich, you're going to have to get a job. Even if you were born rich, I recommend it. We required our kids to get jobs. The first couple jobs you get will certainly not be your dream job but you will learn, hopefully, life lessons in dealing with other employees, management and of course learning to listen to customers' (real people) needs and what the world is really like. It doesn't matter how crappy the job is, and your dumbass friends might make fun of you but it's just a stepping stone of knowledge you're gaining in life's lessons and a few bucks on top of that. Oscar Wilde said, **"Experience is simply the name we give our mistakes."** You will probably make mistakes working for others, but you will learn something too, I hope.

> **"Opportunities are usually disguised as hard work, so most people don't recognize them." Ann Landers (1918 – 2002) American columnist**

The first lesson is that you must start saving money from day one, the first paycheck. This is a habit you must learn to commit to. It's your money, and if you put a certain amount or a certain percentage in the bank every pay-day starting with the first check, you won't ever miss it. Consider it locked up for your safekeeping and budget the rest of your money as you see fit. Remember the "Pay yourself first theory" in chapter 1?

It is generally well known that Americans have become terrible savers and terrific spenders. We take on too much debt. Many American households live paycheck to paycheck because they spend their money before they earn it (mostly credit card debt and car loans). Nearly half of Americans couldn't cover a $400 emergency expense without borrowing money, according to a recent Federal Reserve report. Currently, Americans have over $1 trillion in credit card debt and $1 trillion in auto loans. Many economists say that unless Americans change their spending habits and learn to save, we will soon have a disastrous retirement crisis.

We are not alone in this crisis, other English speaking countries like the UK, Australia and New Zealand share similar circumstances. Recently, on a trip to Australia, our driver told us that banks in Australia now require home mortgage applicants to demonstrate their *ability to save* money to get the loan. The applicants must show a couple of year's worth of bank statements that show a habit of saving money monthly and hence the source of funds (not from Mom and Dad) for the down payment. The idea being that if the applicant can't save money on a regular basis, how can they expect the borrower to make payments on their loan regularly?

In the Fiji Times, I read that **ANZ Bank** is delivering the "Money Minded and Business Basics" across the country which brings financial literacy training to youths. "Savings takes away that payday to payday living and existence. Young people learn saving habits early so that when they want certain things for their lives they will save for it rather than going to borrow money. While we are a bank *and we make money* from lending money... we strongly feel that people should borrow money for good (things) and that borrowing money isn't the answer to everything. Everyone should have an emergency fund", said Mrs. Joanne Stewart, head of retail banking at ANZ, quoted in Fiji Times 2/28/19.

Island Pacific Academy in Kapolei, Hawaii, partnered with HawaiiUSA Federal Credit Union to set up an on campus credit union where elementary students could learn financial skills and save money, Honolulu Star Advertiser, 5/7/19. Fourth grade students operate Navigator Credit Union on campus every Wednesday, thirty minutes before school starts.

So far, they have racked up forty accounts and over $20,000 in deposits from classmates!

Other countries, such as Japan, have a savings culture that is built into the idea that a percentage of each paycheck gets automatically saved, regardless of amount. When I worked at the major aircraft company in the 1970's the Japanese-American women in my department uniformly saved 15 percent of their net pay! This was accomplished through weekly automatic deposit into the credit union savings account there. They never missed the money because they got used to living on whatever was left. I was astounded to learn that since they weren't married yet and living at home, that this savings habit was expected of them by their families and culture. When 401K's automatic withdrawal came along, they did that too *in addition* to their usual credit union savings withdrawals.

America was not always a culture of debt. I know my grandmother never had a credit card and paid cash or check for everything. She always had dough. As I mentioned before, my folks had multiple credit cards and rarely had cash. They lived paycheck to paycheck for many years.

The ultimate goal of Americans was always home ownership but the Holy Grail is financial independence. Brian O'Connell, writing for THE STREET, 7/23/18 had this to say in Daily Ideas for Saving Money: "Take the 52 week challenge. Here, the idea is to save $1 the first week, $2 the second week, $3 the third week, and so on, until the last week in the year which is $52. Do that every week, and you'll save $1,378 over the entire year." The idea is to show you how easy it is to create a savings habit that you get used to and realize just how easy saving can be. Remember the "how do you eat an elephant" metaphor in chapter one?

There was an article in MONEY by Abigail Abrahms, 8/1/17, that says: Millenials are outsaving Gen Xers in one department: retirement savings. This is because US employers have made changes in the last decade that make it easier for employees to participate. Auto-Enrollment in retirement accounts when they get hired into a job makes the decision much simpler and the employee doesn't miss it.

In Hawaii, where in 2020 one in four residents will be over 60 years old as the "Silver Tsunami" comes rolling in from the oldest of the baby boomers start hitting their early 70's. Currently the senior poverty rate is 17 percent, the sixth highest in the nation. The **Hawaii Saves** proposal is currently being debated and is modeled after the **Oregon Saves** program. Through that program, the deduction is an automatic 5 percent of Gross pay. The state directs the money to low-cost investment funds and it's mostly designed for those who don't have company provided 401K's is my understanding such as the self-employed. Australia has started something similar called the Superannuation Guarantee Compulsory Program to encourage people to accumulate retirement savings. The point is that they all see danger on the horizon for massive numbers of people who never managed to save a nickel for retirement. That's why they're trying to come up with programs to save people financially by helping them save money.

"I am not a product of my circumstances. I am a product of my decisions." Stephen Covey

Why are all these countries and states creating these programs, you ask? Because this generation of retirees, the Baby Boomers, is coming to retirement age with a large population of people with little or no savings, certainly not enough to carry them through the years after retirement. Many Americans expected Social Security to be their retirement plan and carry them through the "golden years". The generations after them never learned to save either and are arguably even worse savers.

A little about Social Security here: The Social Security act (SSA) was passed August 14, 1935 as "An act to provide for the general welfare by establishing a system of Federal old-age benefits". President Franklin Roosevelt in a speech said "The Act does not offer anyone, either individually or collectively, an easy life nor was it ever intended to do so. None of the sums of money paid out to individuals in assistance or in insurance will spell anything approaching abundance. But they will furnish that minimum necessity to keep a foothold; and that is the kind of protection Americans want". (On the third anniversary of the SSA, August 15, 1938.)

Basically, this is saying that Social Security benefits are supposed to **supplement** your own retirement savings and to keep you from starving if you have none. Well that's certainly not the retirement *I* want to plan for. Unfortunately, a recent study by the Federal Reserve found 25 percent of working Americans have no retirement savings and another study showed that 9 percent of seniors lived in poverty in 2017 which would have been 39 percent if it wasn't for Social Security. Additionally, the funds that were originally deposited in SSA were locked up but later presidents convinced congress to put the funds in the general fund which they spent immediately of course. There have been discussions about Social Security going bankrupt ever since. In 1982 Ronald Reagan and Tip O'Neill increased taxes and raised the retirement age to create a trust fund to help save Social Security. This trust fund was supposed to be a buffer to allow politicians enough time to figure out a permanent solution. Nothing has happened since 1982 and in 2020 the program will start drawing from the trust fund to keep it going. If Congress does not act, there will be significant cuts to benefits starting in 2034. So, bottom line, don't count on it being there when you retire fifty-two years from now. Save your own money so you don't have to worry about it.

But you, being a teen, think of retirement age as something so far off in the future that you can't fathom that. I know I never thought about it when I was your age.

WHAT YOU NEED TO KNOW: A Social Security number is a 9-digit string of numbers that should not be shared with anyone else so it is your very own. Everyone needs a Social Security number nowadays. You need it to get a job, open a bank account, get loans or credit cards (that's one big reason you don't share it) besides being able to pay taxes. It is also used to get your credit scores. Even noncitizens who want to work in the United States can get a number (if they have legal authorization to be here) from the Social Security Administration office. This is how immigrants can legally get jobs and pay taxes. If you need a number for tax purposes only, and you aren't authorized to work in the United States, you can apply for an *Individual Taxpayer Identification Number* (**ITIN**) from the Internal Revenue Service (IRS). Whatever your legal status is, you're going to need a Social Security or ITIN number so Social Security taxes can be taken out of your paycheck.

The whole point of this chapter is to convince you to save money towards your goals instead of borrowing money for *stuff*. You could have multiple accounts for different goals like a college fund, a vacation fund, or down payment for a house fund, a car or even ***an investment property opportunity*** fund. The savings plan you create could be the beginning of your great accumulation of wealth. Your savings will be there when that once in a lifetime deal comes by as well as that unexpected catastrophe like mine in chapter 2. As the Boy Scout motto says, "Be Prepared". We really wished we had a load of money in the bank when the recession hit in 2008. Yes we had *some* cash, of course, but not enough to pick up some juicy real estate opportunities. Most of our money was already tied up in real estate. Someone once said that the saddest two words in the English language is "if only". My wife always says, "Cash is king".

I would suggest these savings from your first few jobs be in a bank or credit union savings account. This would provide you a tiny bit of interest on your deposits but the liquidity to withdraw at a moment's notice (which you won't do I hope). As a teen, I don't believe you need or want a checking or debit account at your age and banks probably won't give you one anyway but you will need to get one eventually when you start paying bills. Some credit unions do offer a "high-yield liquid account" like Hawaii State Federal Credit Union's "Regular Share ($5.00 minimum)" account which has currently 0.25 percent APY. As with most credit unions, larger deposits can command more interest. A minimum daily balance of $25,000 could get you 0.35 percent for example.

Since I began writing this little book, I have been made aware of another new way of saving called Acorns. Basically, this is a debit card that rounds up your debit card purchases to the next dollar and puts the change in a fund account for you. So if your bill comes to $35.25, they put $0.75 into your ETF (Exchange Traded Fund) account and your debit account gets charged an even $36.00. This is micro-investing and a fast and easy way to accrue savings and it is amazing how fast it does grow.

This is the perfect time to bring up another point, the world is constantly changing and new ideas and technologies are coming out all the time which could change people's personal lives and how they conduct business. You need to keep up with what's going on in the financial world as well as all the other new technology and devices that are always coming out.

Even at your age I'm sure you've heard of the exorbitant salaries offered to members of professional sports teams. They collect millions in salaries for their expertise in their chosen game but most have no expertise in saving money or even holding onto it for long. They lose it in a variety of ways such as trusting someone else to take care of their investments, spending money on things like cars, boats airplanes/jets, and of course their "posse" which are usually nothing more than a bunch of parasite yes-men (syco-phants) that the sports celeb parties with and pays for.

Statistics show that 70 percent of lottery winner's end up broke and a third of those eventually end up in bankruptcy.

More than 78 percent of former NFL players are broke or financially stressed after retiring from the game and 60 percent of former NBA players go broke within five years of retirement. Baseball players and Hollywood Celebrities are not immune. All of them had one thing in common, they couldn't control their spending, didn't know how to put money away let alone not know how to invest money to make money. If you think about some of the salaries of these so-called "Rich and Famous" they could've bought an entire apartment complex for cash every year and still lived lavishly on their salaries. Then after their retirement sit back and live off the rents. They are the poster children of irresponsible behavior, stupidity and in some cases arrogance.

"Some people are born on third base and go through life thinking they hit a triple" Barry Switzer, famous coach.

That brings us to the question: What do you consider rich or wealthy? What is your definition of a Millionaire?

CHAPTER 6

WHAT IS THE DEFINITION OF RICH, WEALTHY OR MILLIONAIRE?

Before I answer that, let me ask the question: What's the difference between poor and broke? Someone along the line once told me, "Poor is a state of mind. Broke is a financial condition." In other words if you think of yourself as poor you're right (remember chapter 1) and there is nothing you can do about it. If you realize that you're just broke, you have a different opinion of yourself, your conditions and your options. You make a plan on how to change your financial conditions and work it, like maybe getting a job for example. You know you have options. The hardest part to overcome is **inaction**. Fear of failure always produces inaction or procrastination.

Many of the bankrupt celebrities and sports players who made millions of dollars and ended up bankrupt had a lot of money when they were working in their careers. I guess you could call them rich or wealthy or even millionaire for a little while then but then after they left the game they were definitely broke when the money ran out. Many of them came from desperate backgrounds as kids growing up in poverty stricken areas of the world with parents who didn't know much about money except for working a job and getting a paycheck. They didn't get the financial education they needed to break out of generational poverty cycle repetition. It's such a shame to see this happen when it could have been prevented and they could've done such great things with their big paychecks when they were coming in. This kind of narcissistic and grandiose behavior is often found in people who actually feel they have no self worth. They feel they need to show flash even if it's leased or rented. I always say "If you can't pay cash for your flash, you're just a pretender".

MUNKnee.com website, August 12,2019 reports that majority of NFL, NBA and MLB players go bankrupt within five years of leaving the game because of 1) Overspending, 2) Career duration, 3) A lack of financial knowledge, 4) Poor investment decisions, and 5) Hanging with a bad crowd.

"Live life with a due sense of responsibility, not as those who do not know the meaning of life but as those who do" Ephesians 5:15

Magic Johnson was one player who was able to think beyond the playing years as Wikipedia writes below:

"**Johnson began thinking of life after basketball while still playing with the Lakers. He wondered why so many athletes had failed at business, and sought advice. During his seventh season in the NBA, he had a meeting with Michael Ovitz, CEO of Creative Artists Agency. Ovitz encouraged him to start reading business magazines and to use every connection available to him. Johnson learned everything he could about business, often meeting with corporate executives during road trips. Johnson's first foray into business, a high-end sporting goods store named Magic 32, failed after only one year, costing him $200,000. The experience taught him to listen to his customers and find out what products they wanted. Johnson has become a leading voice on how to invest in urban communities, creating redevelopment opportunities in underserved areas, most notably through his movie theaters and his partnership with Starbucks. He went to Starbucks CEO Howard Schultz with the idea that he could successfully open the coffee shops in urban areas. After showing Schultz the tremendous buying power of minorities, Johnson was able to purchase 125 Starbucks stores, which reported higher than average per capita sales. The partnership, called Urban Coffee Opportunities, placed Starbucks in locations such as Detroit, Washington, D.C., Harlem, and the Crenshaw District of Los Angeles. Johnson sold his remaining interest in the stores back to the company in 2010, ending a successful twelve-year partnership. He has also made** investments in urban real estate through the Canyon-Johnson and Yucaipa-Johnson funds. Another major project is with Chicago.

Johnson runs Magic Johnson Enterprises, a conglomerate company that has a net worth of $700 million; its subsidiaries include Magic Johnson Productions, a promotional company; Magic Johnson Theaters, a nationwide chain of movie theaters; and Magic Johnson Entertainment, a film studio. In addition to these business ventures, Johnson has also created the *Magic Card*, a prepaid MasterCard aimed at helping low-income people save money and participate in electronic commerce. In 2006, Johnson created a contract food service with Sodexo USA called Sodexo-Magic. In 2004, Johnson and his partner Ken Lombard, sold Magic Johnson Theaters to Loews Cineplex Entertainment in 2004. The first Magic Johnson Theater located in the Baldwin Hills Crenshaw Plaza, closed in 2010 and re-opened in 2011 as Rave Cinema 15.

When I read that Michael Ovitz encouraged him to start reading business magazines and learn everything he could about business it kind of reminded me of my story at the beginning of this book where my mom said "Well I guess you could start by reading the Wall Street Journal". Johnson is currently estimated to have a net worth over $600 million. Way to go Magic!

There's a big difference between making a lot of money and building lasting wealth. The financial education you need for your future may not be found in a class or in attaining a degree for that matter, but you can find it on your own. You can read stories of successful people, talk to people you meet that you think are successful and start getting ideas about how they did it. The worst thing in the world as far as I'm concerned is listening to those dummies in your neighborhood who will never amount to anything anyway especially gang members, dope heads and criminals.

Let's get back to the title of this chapter "What's the definition of rich, wealthy and a millionaire" in the financial sense?

Rich: Having a great deal of money, plentiful, abundant copious.

Wealthy: Having wealth: very affluent, ample (generously sufficient to satisfy a requirement or need).

Millionaire: an individual whose net worth is equal to or exceeds one million units of currency. At the end of 2017, there were estimated to be just over 15 million millionaires in the world (in US dollars). The US has the highest number of high net worth individuals (HNWI's) of any country (5,047,000). Some financial writers say a millionaire is a person with $1 million or more in income. It used to be back in the 1950's, that a "millionaire" was a very wealthy person. Nowadays, any decent house near any California beach city will be close to a million if not more. Of course there's a lot of mortgage (debt) sitting on those assets.

My definition of wealthy is when you no longer *need* to work for somebody else because your investments provide enough passive income every month that you can live comfortably and share with others. Work and investment produce wealth but, investments often pay way more than you could *ever* earn by working.

There are multiple ways of calculating millionaire status. The most common is using "Net Worth". To calculate net worth, take the value of everything you own and subtract the value of everything you owe, the result is your net worth.

So here's a question for you: If you had a million dollars cash, you'd be the definition of a millionaire, right? What if you took that money and bought a $100,000 boat, $100,000 worth of jewelry or a $380,000 exotic luxury car, are you still a millionaire?

The answer is no, you're no longer a millionaire, you're just a silly fool. There is a saying about "You can't have your cake and eat it too".

But wait! What if you took a $100,000 and put it on a down payment on a $1,000,000 mansion or $300,000 for a down payment for a mortgage loan on a $1,500,000 commercial property or apartment building? Are you still a millionaire?

The answer is - **yes!**

Why is that? Because that $380,000 Bentley *lost* value the moment you drove it off the dealers lot. The Rolex watch is no longer worth what you paid for it either, because it's used now. The boat and the airplane are just going to eat up money every month that you own it. (A famous saying is: The happiest two days of a boat owner's life is the day he bought it and the day he sells it).

As to the mansion: Although you will be paying high property taxes on it every year and possibly a larger than average utility and maintenance bill, it should at least hold its value if not increase it in the coming years. Hopefully you have enough income to pay the maintenance expenses and taxes. It would still count as a $1,000,000 asset (worth whatever you paid for it) as far as accounting goes. You still have a mortgage ($900,000) which goes on the liabilities side of your balance sheet. So it still balances out to the amount you put down ($100,000) on your net worth. Of course these days a true mansion will be several million dollars.

The apartment building or commercial property has rent coming in every month (hopefully), every year. You might even get a bump up in rents once in a while. The rent money from the apartment building goes to pay its mortgage payments and hopefully is enough to pay its property taxes and insurance plus put some money in your pocket.

The commercial property rent pays the mortgage also but being a triple-net lease, the renter is responsible for paying you for his share of the property taxes (which does go up sometimes), the cost of insurance, and any maintenance (except maybe the roof). If you priced it right these rental properties will be putting some extra cash in your pocket every month! They are definitely kept on the books as assets and the mortgage owed is a liability on your balance sheet.

Ding, ding, ding! Winner! You're still a millionaire, accounting-wise.

Here's a thought: How much money do you need to be rich? If you were able to lock up $1 million and got 2.5 percent interest per year you'd have $25,000 income before taxes. I hear you say "But that's not enough!" Ok then, lock up $10 million and you'd have $250,000 and so on and so on with each additional zero. The point is if you spend everything on "stuff" and/or credit card interest you end up with nothing.

HOW A MORTGAGE WORKS: Let's say you bought a rental property and the rent is paying the mortgage every month. Every month the bank's (mortgage) payment is made up of two parts: a small amount of principal (the amount you borrowed) and a large amount of interest (the monthly fee the bank is charging you for the privilege of borrowing from them). Think of a mortgage as a loan on a sliding scale, every monthly payment has a little more going to principal and a little less going to interest. The idea is that at the end of the loan period, could be thirty years, the principal owed has reduced to zero and the loan is done, or dead (hence the word mort) and you don't owe any money to the bank anymore. And all this time, someone else has been making the payments for you if it was a rental! This is a wonderful country!

HOW DO YOU GET A MORTGAGE: First, traditionally you can go to a bank or a loan broker and speak to a loan officer or today, with some of these online mortgage lenders. They will analyze how much you make, calculate your net worth (total assets minus your liabilities) and review your credit history/rating. You will tell them *how much down payment* you have and they will determine how much of a loan you qualify for. If you're married at that time, they will analyze your spouse too (using both of your Social Security numbers). Your down payment plus the income you and your spouse have will determine how much you can borrow (are qualified for) which will tell you what price range to look for in a house or condo. The whole purpose of this ordeal is to analyze your ability to pay and your history of paying back debts in a timely manner. Keep in mind that you might want to have a few bucks left over to fix up the place the way you like it or get appliances if they're not included. The bank or lender will also figure out how much is going to be paid for real estate taxes and insurance. If you ask, they will automatically add 1/12 of the amount due for taxes and insurance to your monthly payment and deposit those sums into an escrow account. When the taxes and insurance are due, they will make the payment directly to the county or insurance company for you.

The down payment required can be different with every loan and is usually stated in percentages of the purchase. For example, a $200,000 house would require a 20% down payment for a "conventional loan". In other words, you will have a $40,000 check that you can give the escrow company and the bank would make a loan for $160,000. There's more, Closing Costs. The escrow agent will arrange to pay one year's worth of insurance, escrow fees and other closing costs like title insurance and broker's fees to the realtors involved. Some of these closing costs can actually be negotiated between you and the seller. The lender will most likely add your share of all these costs to the loan.

Additionally, the National Association of Realtors says that 81% of Americans purchase with less than 20 percent down currently. If you don't have 20 percent down, you can still buy the home but the lender may require you to get PMI Insurance which stands for Private Mortgage

Insurance. It helps you qualify for the loan if you otherwise couldn't. It does cost extra each month. You could consider it a penalty for not saving enough to put 20 percent down.

First time homebuyers can get some additional help from Fannie Mae and Freddie Mac which offers them 3 percent down programs. Military veterans can qualify for 100 percent financing through the Veterans Administration (V.A.). Lastly, for certain areas that the U.S.D.A. (Department of Agriculture) has designated it as "rural", 100 percent financing is also available.

Generally speaking, although a home may be the biggest purchase most people will ever make it's not necessarily the *best* wealth building move but it's a great starting point. For example the S&P (Standard and Poors)/Case-Shiller U.S. National Home Price Index shows houses averaged 3.47 percent annual gain over the last 30 years whereas the S&P 500(stocks) averaged 7.63 percent. Additionally, some have said anything that costs you money is not an asset but actually is a liability. Nevertheless, think of each monthly mortgage payment as one bite of the elephant. Heck, you were going to be paying rent somewhere anyway. You may not be getting rich quick but you are accumulating wealth smartly as you pay down the mortgage and your house appreciates in value (we hope).

Lastly, many buyers have made the mistake of buying a house that is actually more than they can afford. The condition is called "house poor" in that it is basically the only asset they have and it soaks up every extra cent they have each month. They can't afford to do much of anything else because they have committed way too much of their income especially if there is a hiccup in their job or the economy in general. Additionally, many people in 2008 found themselves "house poor" when the real estate market collapsed because they couldn't sell their real estate for what they owed on it, a condition known as "upside down" on the property.

TYPES OF INVESTMENTS

What I will be discussing in this section is just a cursory look at types of investments. I never had a class on stocks or the stock market in school because just like anything else having to do with money, the schools don't teach you about it. I had to find out about these on my own which took considerable time, sometimes years. Hopefully these few examples will make the process speedier for you than that was mine.

Except for those who are temporarily millionaires like lottery winners and celebrity/sports stars, what do **all** millionaires have in common? Investments that pay them income! The IRS says that the average millionaire has seven streams of income. That means seven different investments are paying them such as rental property, business ownership, stock dividends or bond interest for example.

Whether its stocks, bonds, commodities, real estate, or their own business' they have invested their money somewhere. Sure, some of them may spend lavishly at times but they don't kill and *eat the goose that lays the golden eggs*, so to speak, by ending their investment. They never do that, not the real millionaires.

Let's think of money as corn or soybean seeds for a minute. The young farmer may have to save up to buy seed (hence the phrase seed money) among other things when he/she first gets started and maybe even rent/lease a farm from someone else (tenant farming, or sharecropping) in order to plant. After harvest is over, and he/she sells his crop, and hopefully has enough to pay back any loans with interest, pay for his equipment, maintenance and labor costs and have enough left over to have made the whole enterprise worthwhile and then some.

So do you think the farmer runs out after harvest and buys Rolex's and Bentley's?

Heck no! After putting aside what he thinks all his living expenses will be next year, he also puts aside "seed money" for next year so he doesn't have to borrow next season which will help him save some interest costs. If you think about it, he gets one paycheck a year from his crop unless he does something on the side like raising hogs year round.

Farming is a calculated risk. There are many factors such as trying to make an educated guess how much corn or soybeans will sell for at the end of next season (October) before you buy the seeds and plant in early spring.

The main point is, he is basically setting aside a certain amount of his crop this year for next year's seed requirements (seed money). By not having to borrow next year will not just help save interest expense but allow for more money to be set aside for future investments like renting more land which will require more seed and more equipment expenses.

So, let's try some math here:

Average farm size in Iowa is 325 acres. Average harvest in Cedar County is 191.2 bushels per acre corn or 64.6 bushels per acre soybeans. If corn is currently selling at $3.645/bu and soybeans are $8.31/bu. How much gross income could he estimate if he planted the whole crop in one or the other grain commodity?

325(acres)	325(acres)
X191.2 corn bu/acre	x64.6 soybean bu/acre
62,140 bu corn	20,995 bu soybeans
X $3.645 price per bu	x $8.31 price per bu
$226,500.30 gross sales	$174,468 gross sales
-$750 (cost of 3 bags of seed)	-$750 (cost of 3 bags of seed)
$225,750.30 gross profit	$173,718 gross profit

You need to subtract all other expenses like rent or mortgages now to come up with Net Profit. So that's it for the year. What would you do now? Buy more seed, rent or buy more equipment and acreage to make even more next year *or* buy gold chains watches and expensive cars? Hmmm? Did you know that a good used combine could cost between $250,000 to $330,000? That's a lot more than most luxury cars.

Hopefully, there were no hurricanes, tornados or droughts before harvest and demand is high next year. Also, note that soybeans are needed to replenish the minerals in the soil that corn extracts out. Hence, crop rotation is needed at some point.

LEVERAGE

Atlas could move the world if he had enough leverage is the old saying.

David could beat Goliath because David knew the power of leverage his slingshot could dispense was much greater than his own physical strength could administer. Such leverage would be similar to Einstein's E=MC squared where E would equal impact energy, M would be the size and weight of the stone and in this case c would equal the speed the stone had just before impact which was created by the centrifugal force of his model slingshot. A real knockout!

We are talking about financial leverage in this case also known as "gearing" in the UK and Australia, is a general term for using borrowed capital (aka money) to make profits that are expected to be greater than the interest and principal payable. Leverage, in the financial world, allows investors to invest borrowed money to maximize returns such as a mortgage. If the bank requires 20 percent down, that's 5 to 1 leverage. Leverage is power that you can use to work in your favor like buying a $500,000 house by only putting $100,000 down. Typically, a fixed rate or adjustable rate mortgage (loan) gives the average person the leverage they need to purchase a home or investment property.

If you don't have any money to put down from your savings, you've got no leverage.

Now, just for a second, do you remember our friend Eeny from Chapter 3?

If you will recall, he put in $1000.00 a month for 10 years and quit after that. Not counting any compounded interest build up he had $120,000.00 sitting in the account.

What if I were to tell you there is a way for someone else to continue to put $1000.00 in that account for him after he had stopped? It could happen if he were to use that $120,000 as "leverage" to put down on a rental or commercial property that had a monthly NET OPERATING INCOME (NOI) of more than $1000.00. NOI, keep in mind, is before the mortgage is paid, but let's not get too complicated yet.

Keeping it simple, you need to become familiar with the word equity. Equity is one of those words that can have multiple meanings such as fairness or unbiased. In the financial world, equity can refer to the common stock of a corporation or in this case, in real estate, the value of ownership in a property over and above all loans or claims against the property. Equity is the difference between what the property is worth if sold and the amount that is owed. In ultimate simple terms, if you were to sell the property and pay off all the loans or tax claims against it, its how much money you would walk away with after paying off all debts. Equity usually increases each month you make a payment on the mortgage because the principal is reduced slightly each month. If you own a house for example, you will make a monthly payment made up of principal and interest. Additional equity is earned if the property value goes up higher than when you bought. What's even better is if you own rental property where tenants *pay you* money to make your mortgage payments.

Also another example of leverage: If you found a way to make 6% interest on an investment of $100 that would be a profit of $6, right? If you borrowed the hundred dollars at 3 percent interest your net profit would be 3 percent or $3 using borrowed money. This is what many corporations do all the time only in millions of dollars.

Consider real estate equity a type of piggy bank that just continues to grow every time you pay your mortgage bill with either your own money or with the tenants rent money. Equity build-up will be a huge part of your net worth. Real estate has always proved to be a way of building wealth in the long run.

The wealth paradox is borrowing money to purchase things like real estate investments or business'. If you get debt that can create more income than the loan payments, taxes and insurance require you have "cash flow". When you have shifted your savings into investments that pay more than the banks pay in interest you have created income. Using your savings to make large real estate purchases is leverage.

CASH-ON-CASH RETURN

Cash-On-Cash Return is the return percentage of annual cash flow compared to the total amount of actual cash invested. Investors use it to quickly calculate the rate of return based on the amount of cash they initially invested from assets that create income. It is typically used to estimate the return (profitability) for a one year period. Here's an example:

An investor is interested in an investment property. This investment property makes $20,000 a year gross annual net income.

If she were to put $100,000 down to purchase the property she would have a 20 percent Annualized Pre Tax income (20,000/100,000).

Everyone knows that expenses will be incurred during any given year of ownership. Expenses could be anything that costs money like maintenance, landscaping or security for example. After you subtract her annualized expenses from pre-tax income and divide that result by her $100,000 initial cash investment, you'll get her Cash-On-Cash Return percentage. Example: $20,000 Annualized Pre-Tax income minus $5,000 estimated annual expenses equals $15,000. $15,000 divided by the initial investment would equal 15% cash on cash return.

Investors use Cash-On -Cash to compare one deal to another when making a decision on which property to invest in. It is a good tool to use **as long as the numbers supplied to you are accurate.**

PASSIVE INCOME

Passive income is another term you need to know. It refers to the money you make from things or investments that pay you without actively working for a paycheck. Some people have called passive income from rentals, interest income from bank accounts and stock dividends "making money while you sleep" or "mailbox money". Hopefully your rental income will be enough to pay the mortgage, taxes, insurance and have a bit left over to cover expenses when a tenant moves out and you wait for the next one to move in. When you get to the point in your financial life where your income from passive investments far exceeds your expenses, you have achieved financial independence.

NEW TYPES OF LOANS

We've already discussed a little bit about mortgages and amortization (how the loan gets paid off). Let's discuss different types of loans and lending.

Beside the usual banks, savings and loans and credit union institutions, new and not so new lenders are becoming popular with the advent of the internet such as "**crowdfunding**". Crowdfunding is where small amounts of money are raised from a large number of people for a specific project. There are three basic characters involved with crowdfunding, the initiator or the guy with the idea to do something, the individual investors and a moderating organization who provides a platform or forum for the crowd-sale. An example of crowdfunding platform sites include IndieGoGo, Kickstarter, GoFundme, Microventures and YouCaring. These have been used for entrepreneurial projects successfully as well as some charitable projects but unfortunately there have been some fraudulent and deceitful characters getting into crowdfunding also. I personally steer clear of participating in crowdfunding because I don't trust it yet. Maybe in a few years I'll change my mind. It reminds me of the pyramid schemes that were prevalent in the 1970's where many of my friends participated and never saw their money again. This conclusion may be a bit unfair but I am just wary of the whole thing at this point even though I know there have been some very successful campaigns for projects.

ANGEL INVESTORS are usually wealthy (aka accredited) individual investors who will provide capital for projects that they believe in or a startup venture that needs seed money. Historically used for Broadway theater productions that needed financing it has migrated onto Silicon Valley startups in large numbers and more recently other industries. This is very similar to crowdfunding in fact angel groups of accredited individuals have recently begun to appear but typically is a single member. The risks are high for the angel investor who many times loses everything, so as you can expect they require a high rate of return and very often include a percentage of ownership. The popularity of angel investing has increasingly been spreading to Canada and the United Kingdom.

SUBPRIME LENDING is typically for people with ultra low FICO scores who are historically late on making payments and can't get loans the conventional way. Subprime mortgages were blamed for the real estate financial crisis of 2008. It's now prevalent with auto loans. Today, people with bad credit or low or no income who have emergencies or financial setbacks have few places to go to other than Payday loan lenders, pink slip lenders and pawn shops. This kind of loan is for people that are high credit risks and are of course going to have higher than average interest rates. I actually once saw a payday lender's contract on someone's used car that was at 96% interest!!!! Can you imagine paying for a car and almost the same amount for interest to boot? These lenders are like the predators picking off the weak and stupid ones in the herd. They justify their higher rates because a higher proportion of these people will end up not paying back their loan.

CHAPTER 7

OWNERSHIP/INVESTING/ (EQUITY) STOCKS

Some have called the stock market the greatest wealth creator ever devised. The "Stock Market" is how shares of companies are bought and sold everyday. The first thing you need to know is what stocks represent and what a "share" is.

To the majority of most high net worth individuals (HNWI) ownership (read investment equity) is a priority. Many have started businesses with partners, co-owners and other investors. Eventually, if and when the business achieves a certain level of success, they will often "go public", sometimes with much fanfare on Wall Street. "Going public" means the company will begin selling equity (shares) to the public in the open market. For example, take any of the latest stock market entrants such as Netflix, Google or Amazon when they had an IPO (initial public offering). By owning more shares than anyone else, the original start-up guys often continue to maintain control of the company but have a lot more co-owners of varying degrees based on how many shares were purchased.

Even if a company is not enormous, they can go public as a "penny stock" with little notice by the public. Even smaller, what is referred to as "mom and pop" level, it could be an S corporation which will be virtually unknown to the general public and not publicly traded.

What is a corporation and a stock?

A corporation is an association of individuals who create a legal entity which becomes the same as *a legal person*. There are way too many different types of corporations to mention here but suffice it to say some have a couple members and some have millions who are referred to as shareholders (or stockholders). There is always a board of directors in charge of making decisions for the entire company. These board members are typically elected or appointed by the shareholders. Each share is equal to 1 vote in an election. One of the directors will be chosen to be chairman or president (or could be both offices combined). (*As an aside, it wouldn't hurt for you to find out about Robert's Rules of Order which instructs how to properly conduct a meeting. Believe it or not, many boards of directors and chief executives have been humiliated at the annual meetings because they don't know how meetings are properly run.*)

A stock, technically and historically, is a piece of paper — now mostly electronic — that indicates a specific number of shares are owned by a certain person or entity. There are two basic ways a company can raise money or capital, selling stock or borrowing by selling bonds. Stocks never have to be paid back whereas bonds (loans) must be paid back at a certain point in the future.

Let's say you and your friend start a company doing (fill in the blank here). After a while, your company is in the black (making money) and you are advised to start an S corporation ("small business corporation") by your financial advisor, taxman or attorney for liability reasons. You each own 50 percent equally and your company is authorized to issue 1,000 shares. To oversimplify at this point, you can each get 500 shares, which represents 50/50 percentage of ownership.

What does this mean? It means the company's ownership has been cut up into 1,000 pieces (shares of stock) and you and your friend and co-owner could each own 500 shares of outstanding stock.

Stock is frequently referred to as equity (ownership) which translates to value of the shares. Total assets minus total liabilities equals shareholders' equity (value). In this hypothetical case, you would own 50 percent of proportional shares in the company's equity. Each of you would own your percentage of equity in *everything* the company has, not just the bank accounts and any assets, but also all any loans or obligations the company has to creditors (liabilities).

What if a second friend wanted in on you and your friend's business? What if this second friend offered your company $1000 for 100 shares? (10 percent of the company's equity)? This money will be carried on the books as "Paid in Capital". What would that do to your equity if you and your friend accepted that new friend's offer? What's the value of your company?

Your second friend is essentially saying he believes your company is worth $10,000. How did he come up with that? He took $1000 (the amount he's offering) and divided it by 10 percent. Ten percent is what 100 shares is equal to (100 shares he wants/1000 shares outstanding). $1000/10%= $10,000 (total valuation of the company). If you and the other shareholder agree on this valuation and sell him a hundred shares, you and the other original shareholder would then each now own 45% equity while the minority shareholder (the person with the least number of shares) has 10% equity. If the minority holder sells half of his shares to someone else it has no effect on the percentage of ownership for the first two shareholders but reduces his percentage to 5% and introduces another shareholder to the company.

So the big companies are doing the same thing only with a lot more details and on a much larger scale. Major corporations have issued tens of millions of shares (see The Coca-Cola Company). If you buy even one share, you have a proportional claim to ownership of that company (you own a piece of it). If you look in The Wall Street Journal (wsj.com), you'll see most stocks are listed in two basic categories: the New York Stock Exchange (NYSE) or the Nasdaq. (The Penny stocks will be listed in the "Pink Sheets" which are found in the OTC Markets Group.) These are all exchanges where brokers can find buyers and sellers to buy and sell (commonly called trading) shares for money. If you open an account with a broker such as Charles Schwab, Etrade or Ameritrade, you can buy or sell (trade) any stock in those listings.

Dividends

Some stocks pay dividends. Dividends are a result of the company making profits (called earnings). After earnings per share are calculated (total earnings divided by the number of shares outstanding=EPS), the board of directors may declare a dividend. (This is optional and not required.) That is, the board of directors decide that of the $x amount of earnings (profits) this quarter, the company should keep some of the money to re-invest and expand the business and divide the remaining amount to the shareholders proportionally as a dividend payment. The dividends declared will be publicly announced, which may look something like this:

Announcement Date, "Owners of record date (also called Ex date), will receive $.51 per share dividend on payment date." **Announced** March 29, 2019, **Ex-dividend** date April 9, 2019, **Payment** date May 1, 2019.

In this case, if you owned this stock on April 9th, you would be paid 51-cents per share you own as of that date and will get paid on May 1. What is interesting to note here is that if you buy this stock on April 8 and sell it on April 10, you'll still get paid $.51 a share on May 1 — even though you no longer own it.

After the announcements are made, you will usually see a slight run up of the stock price and a decrease after the ex-date. This is because some investors follow the dividend companies from announcement to announcement. Companies that pay dividends regularly usually announce and pay every quarter.

One little aside here: Many stocks – such as AT&T, for example – have a plan which allows you to choose not to receive a dividend check but rather divert that dividend money to buy additional shares of their company with little or no brokerage fees automatically called **DRIP** (dividend reinvestment plan). Remember the compounding example from chapter 3? This dividend reinvestment program is a form of compounding. Your dividends are traded for additional shares instead of paying you cash based on the current market price of the stock. Now you have additional shares dropped into your account which will pay you an additional amount of dividends next time which buys you additional shares after that and so on and so on. Money, making money, making money, etc.

The ever perplexing question: How do you know how much a stock is actually worth? The absolute bottom line truth applies not only to stocks, bonds, real estate, art, antique cars and whatever investment you can think of: It's worth what someone is willing to pay for it. This is the absolute answer that Adam Smith would give you, total economic freedom lets the market (buyers and sellers) decide market prices. Part of the evaluation of the market will be a result of "supply and demand". It wouldn't hurt you to look up Adam Smith and the supply and demand theory. It's the basis for the "free market economy" and the entire capitalist system. No pharaoh (except the one Joseph advised), emperor, king, dictator or central government commissar has gotten it right yet when they try to run the economy instead of the public. Smith called it the "invisible hand" in his book, The Wealth of Nations, 1776. I truly believe this is the reason for the overall financial success of the United States, but I digress.

"Price is what you pay, value is what you get." Warren Buffet

To illustrate this is an example: During the financial meltdown of 2008, MGM Resorts International stock dropped from close to $100 a share to under $10. What had changed at MGM? Nothing. After all, they still owned their same properties (assets) and the management remained the same. Their income didn't change much. What changed was strictly the views of the shareholders and the buyers. That would be the time to buy, when a stock is down. (Remember buy low sell high?) I tell you this story to illustrate that stock market prices are "frequently nonsensical", as Warren Buffett has said. There is no mathematical certainty in the stock market.

When it comes to stocks, one method to evaluate is price/earnings ratio. This is referred to in publications as **P/E**. You get P/E by dividing a company's stock price by its last 12 months of earnings per share (**EPS**). If a company's stock is currently selling at $200 and its EPS is $9.25 the P/E would be 21.6 (200/9.25=21.62). Most investors like a lower EPS and some refuse to buy a stock with an EPS higher than 10. EPS will vary company to company and industry to industry. In the end, it still comes down to what people are willing to pay for the stocks share. You will need to see a financial publication (like WSJ) or some online stock posting that actually shows the P/E for each stock so you don't have to figure each one out yourself. Some people do the same type of evaluation using dividends. Analyzing the fundamentals of a company will help you decide which companies are thriving.

When is the time to buy? The above were just some of the ways some investors look at stocks called "the technicals" of a company. Others may look at the competitive advantage and growth potential a certain company has known as "the fundamentals". Another method is to look at the momentum or stochastics of a stock, in other words is the trend line going to peak or bottom out on a stock's chart using two lines: one reflecting the actual value of the of the oscillator for each session, and one reflecting a moving average (average of maybe the last 90 days) line. Because the price is thought to follow momentum, the intersection of the two could mean a shift in momentum is in the works which indicates a buy or sell signal. Momentum refers to how many shares are being bought or sold daily. This technical analysis will reveal moments of strength and weakness. As Charles Payne says, "Fundamentals tell us **what** to buy while the technicals tell us **when** to buy".

I would like to give a warning here: as a beginner, to make it ultimately simple, you can do two things in the stock market and that is you can buy or you can sell. You could "borrow" against your stocks by "buying on margin" which allows you to buy stocks with money you don't have and can be seriously dangerous financially and way beyond what a 13 year old needs to know at this point. That being said, a number of you rank amateurs can get it right the first time. The odds are less than 50/50 of winning by pure chance. If you should complete a winning trade, please don't be lulled into thinking you are some kind of stock market genius. Many people including myself have been fooled into mistaking pure luck for skill. When the truth comes out at the end, the lessons are expensive. Very often a meteoric rise ends in a disaster stemming from unwarranted overconfidence. I have lost a lot of money in the stock market, especially in the beginning.

Please, do not go out and buy stocks after reading this. Begin studying the market, talk to people in the know, watch the business channel's once in a while (don't go crazy by only watching business network's 24/7). Whatever you do, don't take stock market recommendations from friends or neighbors blindly, investigate for yourself. And most of all, from personal experience, don't do what I did at 13 and take all of my savings from working all summer and invest in stock recommendations from a doctor. No offense to doctors, but historically they have a horrible reputation for making bad investments (lol). Thanks for trying to help me though, Dr. Feigin. You were a great guy. By the way, not only did I eventually lose every cent of my modest investment then but I actually was to repeat this mistake 40 years later with a tip from another doctor on an IPO, but I digress. Back then, in 1965, if you wanted to buy stocks you had to go to a brokerage firm to open an account. With my plan in my head, my stock tip from Dr. Fegin and cash in my pocket my mom and I rode the bus to downtown Los Angeles and went to one of the more famous brokerage houses at the time. At that time, it turned out I could not own stocks in my own name because of my age and so my mom's name had to be on the title as "custodian for" me. That took some of the excitement out but I went ahead with it anyway. In those pre-internet days, unless you had a ticker tape machine in your house like multi-millionaires did, you got your stock quotes out of the newspaper. This was slow and delayed. Unless you called your broker you would never get an up to the minute report. Additionally, in my case it turned out that because my mom was the custodian on title for me, I couldn't just call the broker up and tell him to sell. *Oh no*, I would have to take mom in person (even after I turned 21) in order to sell those shares. That diminished much of the passion I had at the time for stocks but not entirely.

Today things are much different. You can have an online brokerage account get up to the minute stock prices and make buy or sell decisions sitting at home. Not only that, the online brokerage houses today charge a flat fee for trades compared to commissions based on a percentage of the total sale like my first trade was.

Although I eventually lost everything on that stock, I was in the game and I read The Wall Street Journal and the business section of the L.A. Times on a regular basis. What I have learned is that you just can't throw a dart at a chart of stocks and pick one that'll go up in value making you money when you sell. I also learned how the stock market can be influenced and manipulated by outside sources such as inflation or government actions that at first glance seem totally unrelated to your stock.

Although I am still not that passionate about stocks, I still do a few trades now and then mostly in the options market.

"When I was a kid, my father told me there are two kinds of people in the world: smart people and wise people. Smart people learn from their mistakes and wise people learn from somebody else's mistakes", Jim Paul, What I Learned Losing a Million Dollars.

"How do you make a million dollars in the stock market? Start with two million", Old Joke

Instead of picking a single stock that you think might increase in value over the next 12 months, there is a way you can invest in hundreds of stocks all at one time called index funds. The S&P 500 index fund is an example. When you buy one share, it's like you bought a tiny piece of the 500 companies it's made up of. The S&P (Standard and Poor's) is a published list of the 500 largest publicly traded companies in the U.S. It is generally regarded as a representative measure of how the American economy is doing. Other companies like Dow Jones Industrials, NASDAQ and Russell 2000 do similar reports. All of the various reports reflect the general health of the current economy and are used by investment advisors to make recommendations to investors and business planners.

If you contribute to a savings plan, like a 401k or IRA, most often the money is invested in mutual funds which is a conglomeration of stocks similar to the S&P 500 in that its hundreds of stocks that are grouped by categories. As you will find out in case you don't already know, the stock market goes up and down almost daily. If you contribute on a regular basis, say every paycheck, it doesn't really matter what the stock market did this week or month or even this year because as it bounced around your investment bought at the highs as well as the lows. This is called *dollar cost averaging*. In fact, when the stocks went down, your consistently same amount of weekly investment was actually able to purchase more shares than when the market was high. Nevertheless, your number of shares continues to grow with each paycheck deduction.

BONDS

Bonds are different than stocks and there are many types of bonds including corporate bonds, government bonds, municipal bonds (tax free and double tax free) for example.

Bonds are not ownership in a company or entity, they are actually loans. Should the company go bankrupt, bonds are one of the first things a bankruptcy court would order the bankrupt company to pay among a long list of other creditors. After paying all creditors and lenders and bond holders off, anything left would be divided up among the shareholders (stockholders).

The riskier the company is, the more interest it pays. Corporate bonds typically pay the most interest currently between 3-6 percent. Municipal bonds usually pay the least, *but* the interest they pay is usually not taxable.

The other odd thing about bonds is if you purchased a bond at a certain interest rate and then interest rates go up, the value of your bonds (if you wanted to sell) just went down. If interest rates go down, the selling value of your bonds just went up. Either way, your bonds continue to pay you the same amount of interest for the term of the bond as promised, it's just that if you wanted to sell that the price changes.

ANNUITIES

An annuity is actually a type of insurance financial product primarily used by retirees to provide monthly payments over a period of time like twenty years or more commonly the remaining lifetime of the annuitant. It is usually created by making a lump sum deposit and typically ends upon the death of the annuitant although there are multiple variations of continuations. Think of it as a single pay insurance policy that pays you monthly payments till you die. The younger you are the less you'll receive monthly for the same amount of initial investment.

REITS

Another kind of investment is Real Estate Investment Trusts or REITS. REITs are companies that buy multiple commercial properties or apartments which you can buy shares of just like a mutual fund. They may own dozens of commercial or retail properties, apartment complexes or even shopping malls and hold them in trust for their investors. They basically make their money for their investors through the rents. The investors receive a monthly check which is considered "passive income". REITs tend to follow the real estate cycle which typically lasts more than a decade. Stock and bond markets cycle five to six years on average. Delaware Statutory Trust's (DST's) are another type of REIT

BANK ACCOUNTS AND HOW TO PAY FOR STUFF

Banks have evolved over the last thousand years but especially in the last two decades. There used to be banks, savings and loans, and credit unions. Today you can do your banking almost anywhere from automated teller machines (ATMs) and even open and close accounts online without ever visiting a physical branch office. The basic thought for years was that you had to have a checking account to deposit your paycheck or whatever into in order to be able to write checks to pay your bills. At the end of the month, you'd receive a statement which showed a balance at the end of day on a certain date which would be the same date every month or close to it depending on weekends or holidays. The balance shown did not necessarily mean you have that much in the bank. This required you to reconcile the bank statement using a form on the back of the monthly bank statement. For example, the statement says Ending Balance $197.34. The statement will list all of the checks you have written for the month (*that they know about!*) and have paid. You would have kept a record of every check you wrote in your own register (some checkbooks actually have carbon copies of each check you wrote). First, you double check that their list of checks and amounts of each match what your check register is saying. Then you figure out what checks you wrote that the bank had no idea about at the time they printed the statement and make a list of them and the amounts.

Let's say they don't show check number 101 that you wrote to your cousin Marlene for a birthday present on the 6th last month for $25.00. This is because Marlene hasn't cashed it as of the time of the statement printing. So now you take the $197.34 balance the bank is showing and subtract the

$25.00 in order to get the "adjusted" balance of $172.34. But wait, there's more! Since this statement was printed, you made a deposit of $50.00 and wrote a check for $17.35. Now you add $50.00 to the $172.34 and subtract the $17.35 leaving you with $204.99. This is the true amount of money you currently have in your account (also known as reconciled balance).

Today, it's a little different but basically the same idea. Today, using a debit card takes the money directly out of your account in real time rather than waiting for an actual person to take your check to their bank to make their deposit and wait until it clears (gets paid) at your bank. Nearly everything that was once strictly paper has since gone mostly paperless.

Another recent innovation is that you can make a deposit by using your cell phone or other mobile device and your bank's app by taking a photo of the check you're depositing.

What happens if there isn't enough money in your account to pay for the check presented (the bill)? Well, in the old days there were no ATM or cash machines. If you wrote a "bad check", your bank would return it to the bank it came from (Marlene's bank for example) and they in turn would send it back to the person or business that deposited it with them and subtract it from their checking account. Your bank would charge you a "return" fee, like $25.00 for screwing up and deduct that fee in real time. This makes your balance less than what you think it is (they will inform you by mail) and if you didn't know about the $25.00 fee being deducted, you might be accidentally writing another "bad check" because of it. If it turns out you were writing these "bad checks" sometimes called "bounced checks" intentionally, you would be looking at some serious jail time. Meanwhile the guy you wrote the bad check to (perhaps it was to your landlord) will be notifying you and charging you a late fee (maybe $75) and a bad check fee (maybe $25) also.

Sometime in the 1980's or 1990's banks came up with a thing called check overdraft protection. For a fee, (mine is $12 a year) if you had the misfortune of accidentally writing a bad check (or overdraft as the bank calls them), the bank's overdraft protection plan would kick in and pay the check or checks presented, up to a certain limit like $3,000.00 maximum. Your bank would also charge you a fee like $30 for each check they had to cover plus interest each month till you paid off the overdraft account (think of it like a special charge card, an expensive one) in full. This could happen if your tenants check "bounced" and now you don't have as much money in your account as you thought.

Nowadays, there is another slight change in that your debit card could be attached to your checking account as well as a Visa or MasterCard. If you don't have enough in your account you could charge it to your credit card. Again, *there are fees*. ATMs charge a fee for each transaction and depending on where and what ATM you're using fees could range from 50 cents to $5.00 per transaction. If you use your debit card at some places like Starbucks they charge you 50 cents a transaction. Think about it, if you got coffee using your debit card every day for thirty days, you would be spending $15.00 a month just for the privilege of buying coffee with your debit card. If you used the credit card for a cash advance, you would once again likely be charged fees for that privilege.

The Consumer Financial Protection Bureau (consumerfinance.gov) is currently reviewing the 2010 Federal Reserve Board "overdraft rule" which regulates how banks charge fees when their customers spend more money than they have available in their accounts. The current rule requires the bank to get permission before charging a penalty for the overspending from debit card or ATM withdrawals. If the customer chose to opt in for overdraft protection the bank approves the purchase or cash withdrawal and then, on top of that, charges a fee, if not they decline the transaction. These charges, at $30 a pop, add up quickly. Additionally, some banks will re-order the sequence of charges in one day. Instead of sequencing the charges from the earliest to latest time they were charged to sequencing them from highest to lowest. Imagine you had $100 in your account, theoretically, you could make ten $10 purchases in the morning using the debit card right? But, what if then you purchased something for $110 later in the day after that last $10 charge knowing that you've got overdraft "protection" coverage, how many $30 overdraft fees would you expect? One? NO! As I said, some of these banks will re-sequence the charges from highest to lowest for that day so you'll get eleven $30 charges! $330!

You'll notice there are all kinds of fees and charges connected with your checking/debit account including a monthly fee just for the pleasure of banking with them. Some banks don't charge a fee if you maintain a certain balance of all your accounts, checking and savings. I keep a $1000 in a savings account with a horribly crappy interest rate at a bank that I write most of my California checks from just so I don't get charged a $25 monthly fee on my checking account. If you don't maintain the "low minimum balance" your checking account will get charged the standard monthly checking fee which is $25. Also note that banks do not pay you *any* interest on checking accounts. There also might even be an annual fee for the privilege of using the Master Card part of your debit card.

You will only get paid interest on savings, money market and certificate of deposit (CDs) accounts at banks. Credit unions are another story. They pay interest on checking, savings, money market and CD accounts. The interest rate they pay is usually way better than you can get from a bank. Not only that, the interest rates they charge on loans are usually cheaper than banks.

SAVINGS ACCOUNTS AND HIGH YIELD SAVINGS ACCOUNTS

Savings accounts are meant to be a vehicle where you can put some money aside to save for a short term goal. The interest is usually not very much (like .07 percent) in fact right now in some European countries they are charging a negative interest! In any case, you've got to start somewhere, right? The idea is that you won't be writing checks or making numerous withdrawals every month, although the funds are available at any time to withdraw.

Money Market Accounts

Money Market accounts pay higher rates than savings accounts but come with some restrictions such as how many withdrawals you can make a month.

Certificate of Deposit

Certificate of deposits (CD's) are another way to "park" your money for a given period of time (usually a year or more) and are therefore more restrictive. CD's pay more interest than regular savings accounts and money market accounts. The glitch is that you are promising to leave the deposit alone and not touch it for a stated period of time in return for those higher interest rates or else pay a penalty for early withdrawing. Time periods are usually one year or more with interest rates increasing the longer the term. A minimum stated amount of deposit will be required for example a minimum of $1,000 to open the account.

I just realized that I may have taken for granted that you already knew but just in case you didn't know, something I haven't mentioned is that when you see interest rates posted for savings accounts, CD's or even loans, it's always *annual* interest that is stated. So if you see an advertisement for a one year CD at 2.2 percent with a minimum deposit of $1,000, it's 2.2 percent for the entire year. If you see another advertisement for a *two year* CD at 2.4 percent for a $1,000 minimum, its 2.4 percent the first year which would become $1,024.00 after one year and then 2.4 percent on top of that (there's that compounding again) for the second year for a grand total of

$1048.57 at the end of the second year. In any case, you're locked into the time frame you selected when you opened the CD account or pay a penalty.

Here's the dilemma: If you want to park some money for a while but you're not sure what interest rates are going to do in the future (they can only do one of three things: go up, go down or stay the same) you don't want to tie up your money and miss out on possible interest rate increases next year by putting them in a 5 year CD. On the other hand, if rates go down, lower than your current CD rate, you'll be sitting pretty getting more interest than anyone else who signs up for a CD after the rates dropped. Also, maybe you're not entirely sure, but maybe you'll need some of that money next year or the year after.

The solution to this dilemma is doing what is called a **CD Ladder**. Let's say you've got $5,000 to put into a CD. You could put $1,000 in a one year account, another $1,000 in a two-year account, another $1,000 in a three year account, another $1,000 in a four- year account and the last $1,000 in a five-year account. Each year you would be cashing out one account while the rest are still working for you. If rates have gone up next year you can reinvest that money from the first maturing account in another CD at the new higher interest rate. The idea is if you want to keep some of your cash liquid, setting up CD's with different maturity dates creates your ladder. Saving long term in a CD sounds safe and secure, which it is, but the one caveat to keep an eye on is the danger of inflation. Think of inflation as a tax on what you have saved that eats away at the value of your savings. If inflation goes to 5 percent for example and you're earning 2 percent, you actually lost money. Yes, you got your original investment back plus the 2 percent gain, but your purchasing power went down giving you a 3 percent net loss.

GOLD AND SILVER

Eventually, I strongly suggest you purchase some gold and silver. I'm sure you've seen the innumerable commercials on TV advertising gold and silver and wonder what the heck are these guys trying to say. I'll try to explain this way: A one ounce gold coin today is worth a one ounce gold coin a thousand years ago if you go back in time, you'd get an even trade. One paper dollar today is not worth what a paper dollar was twenty-five years ago, let alone a hundred years ago. One gold coin in the early seventies was worth less than $50 in paper money but in the late seventies it was worth over $1200, back down to under $800 in 1990, currently its close to $1500.

Now here's a thought: If you bought a gold coin and the dollar goes down in value you can trade or exchange your coin for more paper dollars than you paid for it. If the dollar went up in value your coin would be worth less paper dollar value than you paid for it. Typically, if we have high inflation like we did in the late 70's early 80's gold prices go up. When inflation went down so did the price of gold.

It can be confusing, I know, but you'll understand eventually as you start watching the market. I know this subject was never brought up in my high school economics class, so I encourage you to research on your own for more understanding. The main thing I want to stress is that gold and silver are not exactly investments. They don't pay dividends, they don't pay rent and they don't multiply like rabbits on their own. They just sit there, in your safe until the next time you take them out and look at them, kind of like a coin or stamp collection. They are what is referred to as a hedge against inflation. Inflation, meaning that it will cost more paper dollars to buy the same product tomorrow than it did today. Dollar down, gold up is the generally accepted theory.

When you are ready to purchase gold or silver my recommendation is you buy an American Gold Eagles. There are Canadian Maple Leafs, Australian

Kangaroos, South African Krugerrands, Chinese Pandas and more to choose from. If the world turned upside down and you needed to pay for basic necessities with your gold, an American coin would be more readily accepted and trusted than an exotic one. Also, I recommend various size coins including the smaller ones in case the people you're dealing with in the future can't make change. I personally do not purchase gold bullion or bars of gold. I do have some silver bullion and several antique silver coins. Many strategists recommend buying "junk silver" which is a name given to silver coins that are too worn to be worth anything to a coin collector, but still contains the weight and purity of the silver inside it. They are sold in bags of $1,000 face value (like 4,000 quarters for example). Each bag will contain approximately 715 ounces of silver that way, regardless of denomination.

CRYPTO CURRENCIES

Cryptocurrency is being touted as the currency of the future. An evolution of currency if you will.

> "Virtual currencies, perhaps most notably Bitcoin, have captured the imagination of some, struck fear among others, and confused the heck out of the rest of us. "
> Thomas Carper, US Senator

Bitcoin was the original cryptocurrency and was an accidental offshoot of another invention. Satoshi Nakamoto, *if that is his real name*, is still unknown other than the inventor of Bitcoin. The system has no central entity, which is actually one of its claims to fame, and instead is a form of network file sharing.

> "Cryptocurrencies leverage blockchain technology to gain decentralization, transparency, and immutability."
> Ameer Rosic, blockgeeks.com

If you can understand that, then you're already a lot smarter than me! The thing is I don't believe most cryptocurrency owners totally understand it either. I have a general rule that if an investment can't be explained clearly in fifteen minutes I will not invest in it. I'm totally suspicious of anything I can't totally understand but my son and others convinced me I should put some money into crypto's. This reeks of "herd mentality" decision making and that's when you need to be most careful.

Today, there are multiple cryptos to choose from: Bitcoin, Ethereum, Litecoin and also their offshoots Bitcoin Cash, Ethereum cash, Kyber Network, XRP and Stellar Lumens (I don't even know what these last three are). There are dozens more that I also don't know about. James Altucher says in his **Crypto-Currencies 101** that there is "close to 1,000 cryptocurrencies out there, about 91-95 percent are complete Ponzi schemes and will eventually go to zero". I currently only have Bitcoin Cash, Ethereum and Litecoin investments. My personal investment is not significant and my son has more invested in crypto's than I do!

I use a company named **Coinbase** to purchase and sell my cryptos. Because cryptocurrency exchanges have had problems with hacks and data breaches resulting in thefts of millions of dollars, I would recommend you use a secure company like them to handle the transactions. Coinbase and Kraken are cryptocurrency exchanges that make buying and selling easy. You can use PayPal or online banking to pay for your transactions with these exchanges. You can let the exchanges hold your investments or you can get your own "Hot Wallet" which will allow you to store your investments on your computer or smartphone. I prefer to leave them at the exchange but know people who insist on keeping them in their "hot wallet". There are other types of wallets also available, but I am not able to comment on them because of my limited knowledge on the subject.

The major thing to remember about cryptos, much like gold, is that the number of paper dollars needed to purchase will fluctuate up and down depending on the market price. Market price in this case will be affected by the number of people trying to buy and sell (trading) dollars for Bitcoins, for example. If a great number of people lose confidence in the dollar, for example, and buy Bitcoin, the number of paper dollars it costs to purchase a Bitcoin will go up (again the supply and demand theory by Adam Smith).

Additionally, although the dollar or the yen may be subject to government manipulation for political reasons, crypto's are immune (so they say).

Crypto's are not my forte' and I am not that competent to either explain or advise on any aspect of them but I do know they seem to be attracting more interest by the general public every year. Facebook is even coming out with a Cryptocurrency called Libra.

"A man's got to know his limitations" Clint Eastwood, Dirty Harry

Welcome to 2020 and Digital Wallets

A lot has happened in the last fifty-four years since I started my quest in regard to banking and paying bills. Checks are passe' as new innovations have been created to pay bills. Of course you can still pay bills "online" from your checking account but other curious methods developed. For one thing, when the internet was invented, it launched a whole deluge of online services, some of which were total pipe dreams that speculators in herd mentality invested millions of dollars into worthless stock. The bubble burst and we had the famous "Dot Com" bust in the stock market cir. 1999. A few of the survivors or successors actually continued on and made a profit. Ebay and Amazon were two that I remember at the time. The next thing I remember changing was that you could buy stuff on Ebay using a credit card or a thing called PayPal. PayPal was a new system that allowed you to buy or sell something online and have the funds withdrawn or deposited into your PayPal account. You could let these funds stay (languish) in your PayPal account or have them eventually transferred into your bank account. The idea was that if you let them sit in your PayPal account, you could use that money to purchase something else on Ebay thereby totally eliminating the need to involve your bank in the transaction. PayPal could also link to your checking account like an ATM card or link to your credit card and charge directly to your credit card account like a common credit card purchase.

Amazon followed suit if I recall correctly and picked up on the PayPal method of payment. This was followed by other companies who either bought or sold stuff online.

Additional ways to pay or transfer money have developed since then such as Venmo. Venmo account holders have to maintain a balance to be used in transactions to transfer funds to others via a mobile phone app which can be linked to bank accounts, debit cards or credit cards. Linking to your bank account or debit card is free but payments using credit cards have a 3 percent fee for each transaction and the credit card provider may charge a cash advance fee. Both the sender and receiver must have Venmo accounts so transfers can be almost instantaneous.

Another convenient way to pay friends and family is through Zelle which is powered by the Chase Banking app. Again like Venmo, both recipient and sender have to be registered with Zelle although a Chase banking account is not required.

Cash App is another digital wallet that is currently popular and like all the other digital wallets it's a means for transferring money from one to another quickly but it does not substitute as an investment that makes you money.

SUMMARY

So basically we've been discussing types of investments. Stocks, bonds, exchange traded funds (ETF's), mutual funds, checking, savings, money market, CD's and REITs', gold, silver, cryptos and real estate. The thing to remember is that it's not all or nothing into one choice. What you want to eventually do is create a diversified portfolio of investments and asset classes. Being young with a long road ahead, you can afford to be a little more aggressive with your various investments than say someone who is nearing retirement and can't afford to lose what they have because they may not have the amount of time left to replace drastic losses.

THE ROAD MAP TO WEALTH

If you want to be successful you'll need to study success. The road map or guidebook to becoming a self made millionaire that I was looking for at age 13 still doesn't exist. Why? Maybe because if it did exist, you wouldn't be a self-made millionaire, you would be a guidebook X follower. You will find that nearly everyone has a different type of personality when it comes to investing. There is no one size fits all formula for everyone and that's actually great because you can follow any route you want and do it anyway you want. There is no one path but each path starts now. You must continually expand your horizons in all directions, be open to change and new perspectives.

"The shoe that fits one person pinches another; there is no recipe for living that fits all cases." Carl Jung, Psychologist

In other words, as I said earlier, this will be an exercise in self education in the world of finances. The fact is, real life is not like in school where they give you tests and there is only one right answer. Also, the teacher usually announces when the next test will be and what the subject of the test will be. In real life, the test date does not come on any predictable date and the subject matter could come out of left field. There are so many variables in real life circumstances that what's right today may not fit the problem tomorrow. One person compared the world of investing to stepping into a smorgasbord buffet where there are so many choices. An old country saying was "There's more than one way to skin a cat,". Donald Trump's book The Art of The Deal was really about how to get what you want in a negotiation. Maybe my mom wasn't wrong after all, like she said, "you could start by reading the Wall Street Journal".

**"You don't get what you deserve, you get what you negotiate."
Donald Trump, Art of the Deal**

"It's not what you've got, it's what you use that makes a difference." Zig Ziglar

Remember, nothing is going to happen until you start making and saving money on your own. Once you have saved some seed money you can start investing. Inaction is the biggest obstacle you will face.

THINGS YOU CAN DO [RIGHT NOW]

- GET TO WORK. Get a job. Learning through experience is just as important as learning from books (remember soft skills?). It doesn't matter what the job is. Learn from your bosses what is important and learn to treat your customers and co-workers with respect. Sears Roebuck had their motto painted on every door that said "Satisfaction Guaranteed" and always instructed employees that the customer was always right, and to make them happy. I don't know that I liked this answer, for example when a certain lady returned a car battery week after week to our catalog store because it had failed after a couple days. I told her nicely that having had a lot of experience with cars, I was pretty sure she had an electrical short in her somewhere in her car, that it was improbable that so many batteries in a row could be defective.

I was merely trying to get her to have the car checked out after this new purchase, I was not denying her return. She threw an extremely loud fit and very nearly cost me my job. "How dare you!" she shouted loudly enough to be heard across the building, "The sign on the door says 'satisfaction guaranteed!" My boss came over and took me in the back room and shaking his finger at my nose, said sternly "First of all, the customer is always right and second, the motto of Sears is Satisfaction Guaranteed." Sears was bought out by Kmart in 2005 and its parent company filed for bankruptcy in 2018. Only six hundred and seventy Sears stores were still operating in 2017 and have continued to close additional stores every year. They had a great reputation for decades and they had been the largest retailer in the USA as of 1990. Many people I know worked at Sears or other department stores such as J.C.Penney's, Macy's or Nordstrom. My wife worked at Robinsons May department store in Beverly Hills where she was so attentive and helpful to customers that many would actually ask for her by name. Mrs. Yul Brenner, for example, would insist on having Pam help her select clothing. Why? Because Pam was the only salesperson honest enough to tell Mrs. Brenner when she tried on various things which items *did not* look good on her. We learned quite a lot about business operations and customer care. Once I suggested to a very negative young man that he get a summer job and suggested he see the manager at the local McDonalds for starters. "I don't want to work at McDonalds for the rest of my life!" he protested. Of course I was not saying to work there the rest of his life, just for a while to get work experience, but he wouldn't listen anymore and stormed off.

- OPENING A SAVINGS ACCOUNT. Head to your bank of choice – or an online-only bank -- and after opening the account put a certain amount in the bank every paycheck consistently.

Forget that it is there and let it build up. As the saying goes, "From little acorns spring mighty oaks".

- DON'T BUILD CREDIT CARD DEBT. Never use a credit card that you didn't pay the entire balance off after you receive the statement before its due date. At thirteen, you don't need a credit card anyway and you're playing with fire when you do get one. The good part is when you do get one, it will help develop your FICO credit score (for better or worse).

- STAY AWAY FROM DRUGS. I always felt like I wasn't as smart as most of my classmates. After seeing some of my "cool" classmates descend into brain damaged fools from drug use, I decided at an early age that I didn't need to handicap myself anymore than I already naturally was when it came to my brain power by losing any additional brain cells. Today, looking at the sheer number of homeless people, many of whom are my age, I can't help but wonder if using drugs in high school started the process of bringing them to the point they are today. I wonder if they were the "cool people" in High School.

> **"If you knew where you were going to be when you die, then chances are you would never plan a visit there."**
> **James Altucher.**

- DON'T BREAK THE LAW. Do not conceive of or participate in an illegal activity to make you money. It's not worth it in the long run. It could result in serious penitentiary time or even in death as happened to a classmate of mine from St. Bernard's High School. Stay away from the crowd that is attracted to illegal activity. It will undoubtedly permanently ruin your life.

> **"Be more concerned with your character than your reputation, because your character is what you really are, while your reputation is merely what others think you are." John Wooden, Coach UCLA**

- GET AN EDUCATION.

"Knowledge is not found in one school",
Hawaiian Proverb.

Whether you get a college degree or not is not what I'm saying necessarily. It could be a trade like plumbing, air-conditioning, or electrician for example. These trades are specialties and pay good money as well as hotel or restaurant management. One of my best friends who has been a major real estate developer in Ohio started off as a union plumber eventually starting his own plumbing business which evolved into creating and building huge housing developments and then re-evolved into building commercial properties like shopping centers. He is a multi-millionaire many times over who barely finished high school. His motto is to treat everyone fairly and squarely, be honest and stand behind your work 100%. Never screw anyone when making a deal.

DO IT YOURSELF. You are the boss of you. God may throw some challenges at you now and then, but you've got to look at each one as a possible blessing. When something totally beyond your control happens, like say a hurricane, you will hear people sometimes say, "Why is this happening to me?" Truth is, I don't know, maybe God is trying to teach you something. The point is that you don't lay down and give up. You get up, dust yourself off, get back to work and figure it out. In my case, in 2017 when Hurricane Harvey decimated my building in Aransas Pass, Texas, I was in shock, disbelief and thought there was a possibility of losing big time. The first couple of bids from reputable construction companies were hundreds of thousands of dollars beyond what I had insured the building for. Thanks to a fortunate, random encounter at City Hall, I met a local contractor, and with the diligence of my wife (best partner in the world) we got the building put back together better than ever with the amount of insurance we had. This was "The Luck Factor" in practice.

- *READ!* Read about people who have gone from nothing to the top all on their own. I have included a list of suggested reading at the end. Read about self-motivation (Tony Robbins), read about making money or investments (Robert Kyosaki) and read about what makes certain people consistently lucky, learned from scientific studies by Dr. Richard Wiseman-Luck Factor.

- GET GOOD AT MATH. You probably won't need to learn calculus and algorithms to make money but believe it or not simple math, fractions, decimals, algebra and percentages make the world go round. You will certainly need to know math if your a tradesman (carpenter, plumber electrician for example) and especially how to read a measuring tape (½,¼,⅛,1/16,1/32 etc.). Someone once told me "You can't be a business owner if you're allergic to math".

- DON'T BE AFRAID TO FAIL. Just like any kind of setback a failure could be a learning experience. Learn from it, get over it and move on. Thats where backup plans and emergency accounts come in handy.

- DON'T FEAR REJECTION. When I worked for the insurance company, the boss, Jim Laurenza, used to say that "maybe only one out of ninety-nine calls may result in a sale but you have to have perseverance so that when you hear "No!", you know you only have ninety-eight more phone calls to go and just keep going". Persistence beats rejection, he was not wrong.

- ACCEPT RESPONSIBILITY. Don't blame others for your mistakes, you're not learning a thing if you do that. Learn to accept blame and how to avoid the mistake next time. I once read that when people interview for a job at Amazon, the interviewer asks about your past mistakes and how you resolved them.

- EXPECT CHANGE. You don't graduate from high school or college and say "I'm done." "Innovate or evaporate" because what worked in the past might not work in the future.

- SAVE MONEY. Be an *investor* not a professional *spender.* Anybody can fall off a turnip truck and be a spender. It's being an investor (saver) that will set you apart from those people who are "all hat and no cattle" as they say down in Texas.

- DIVERSIFY YOUR INVESTMENTS. According to the IRS, the average multimillionaire in the U.S. has seven separate sources of income.

These are just tips I'm giving you here. You need to go out and do it on your own. Doing it yourself is part of the whole experience and will make for great stories when you're my age. The more you manage to handle yourself, the more you will be like forged steel instead of shattered glass.

CHAPTER 8

BEWARE OF EEYORE: THE DOWNERS AND ENABLERS

"Obstacles are things a person sees when a person takes his eyes off his goals" E. Joseph Cossman, businessman and author

Some people you will meet, could be friends or family, will have a case of low self-esteem. They can only feel better about their failures or lack of trying to succeed, by convincing those around them (maybe even you) how impossible the task is. They might have the attitude that something is bound to go wrong no matter what, like Eeyore in Winnie-the-Pooh. Much like the 600lb people we discussed before, every day is a crappy day, life is way too difficult living day to day or paycheck to paycheck let alone setting high goals for the future or even tomorrow. They will speak with such authority as they tell you how hopeless it is for someone like you and mention all the roadblocks that will stop you along the way so you "obviously" can't win. It's like they are trying on the outside to appear helpful and well meaning with advice and guidance but on the inside actually want to diminish your hopes, dreams and goals in order to justify their own lack of self respect and laziness. They might tell you how difficult it is to run a business (even though they never have) or how at your age your dreams are just foolish nonsense, "wait till you're an adult and then you'll see", "it can't be done here" or "it can't be done nowadays", "the best time to invest was twenty years ago." The most hilarious one is when they tell you emphatically that "the taxes will kill you!", as if they know anything about running a business or taxes. Then there's the one about how they had a friend of a friend whose brother-in-law tried the same thing and failed miserably which obviously proves their point (me being sarcastic again). What's even more incredible is that they feel so good after telling you all this negative "advice". The truth, in many cases, is that they suffer from a huge fear of rejection which prevents them from trying.

Others may just want to "help" you by reminding you how incompetent you are by taking away the joy of managing your own funds and "doing it for you" by opening an account for you or holding your money for your own good. By doing this they make you "dependent" upon them as "enablers" to protect you from your own "stupidity or immaturity". This is not what leadership does. Leadership guides people, not controls people. I've always said that you've got to allow people to make mistakes (to a certain degree) because that's how humans really learn. Theoretically speaking, if people accidentally put their hand on a hot stove, they'll never forget it and not repeat the same mistake again.

This negativity is their reality which doesn't allow the possibility of new ideas in. These types of people are not the ones you want giving you business advice let alone life advice. They are usually unable to solve the perplexities of their own lives but somehow always have all the answers for you, which are usually debasing in some way and demoralizing. Also, from experience, never lend money to these people; you'll never see it again. These types of people always seem to be very unlucky.

It doesn't matter if you went to the most expensive school. If your mind is closed and choose not to learn, you won't. Success comes from continually expanding not only intellectually but physically, spiritually and socially.

One thing I learned from the elder care business is not to argue with people with Alzheimer's or dementia because you *can't win an* argument with these people. "You'll never win an argument with them and even if you did manage to convince them, they wouldn't remember twenty minutes from now" is what I used to tell the staff. "Don't waste your breath" I would tell them. The same goes for these downers and enablers. Just be polite, it's not worth your breath arguing with them. They are in their own negative world.

The question remains: Why are they so negative? Why do they have no faith? Why would they want to denigrate or belittle what your hopes and dreams are? Why do they persist?

My answers may not be correct but I have a three point theory:

1. By telling you it can't be done, it's hopeless or no use trying they are actually reflecting on their own lives so that they can't hold ***themselves accountable*** for the decisions (or lack of decisions) they've made in the past. "It's no use, it's hopeless, the cards are stacked against you" ends up being "So why bother?" which then translates to "That's the reason why I didn't bother to try". You must have faith in yourself. If poor people with 8th grade educations can become wildly successful then you can do it too.

2. They want to deconstruct your plan in order to prove it can't work. This again is actually a veiled reproach of their own inability to be able to construct or build *anything* themselves. They are destined to work for others for their lifetime. Remember what Felix Dennis said about two types of work in How To Get Rich? "There are only two types of work in the world, those that change the matter on the earth and those that tell others to do so. The first type is hard work. The second type pays more."

3. They see your faith and hope as a threat to all their beliefs (exposing their excuses) and an insult to their status in life. "How dare you come in here and think individualism, initiative and action can change anything!" The truth is, if there is no hope, why bother with anything constructive? Work ethic, talent and street smarts will kick ass every time.

Addiction is a word you usually hear in regard to alcohol, drugs, gambling or other destructive behaviors. I think many people today are also addicted to escapism. They feel bad about their current life situation and perhaps even guilty for the financial (as well as other) mistakes they've made in the past. They want to try to ignore, forget and justify continuation of more bad decisions such as making purchases that they can't really afford which somehow they think will help make them feel better about themselves to be "hip". In many cases, they truly want to do the right thing but say "I can't" start because their finances are already out of control. Expenses such as exotic vacations or automobiles, renting expensive homes, buying excessive clothes, shoes, jewelry, those "beautifying" piercings and tattoos and other things they really can't afford are just attempts to mask their guilty feelings and destine them to repeating their mistakes. These new mistakes get multiplied by purchasing on credit and not paying off the balance at the end of the month.

If the best time to start was twenty years ago, the second best time to start is today.

What you need around you are people who are of good, positive character who will reinforce your positive attitude, remind you that you *are* capable and to support your desire to achieve your goals. "Birds of a feather" kind of thing. Junior Achievement could be a start. The other kids goals may be entirely different than yours but the social interaction will be an education in itself and many times prove to be fortuitous. DeMolay might be another group for you to investigate. That's where my son learned public speaking. Someone once said "Your friends determine the direction and quality of life." Choose your friends wisely as mentioned before in Proverbs, "He who walks with the wise grows wise".

"Some people get their kicks stompin' on a dream, but I don't let that get me down cause this old world just keeps on spinnin' around" Frank Sinatra, THAT'S LIFE

CHAPTER 9

SO WHAT AND NOW WHAT

"Luck is believing you're lucky". Tennessee Williams

"Extroverts are far more sociable than introverts. Lucky people dramatically increase the possibility of a lucky chance encounter by meeting a large number of people in their daily lives". THE LUCK FACTOR, by Dr. Richard Wiseman

You will not increase your chances of building wealth, businesses or anything else by staying home playing video games in your parent's basement until you're twenty-five years old. "Networking and being open to new experiences will enhance your skills of noticing or creating chance opportunities" R. Wiseman. One study reported that 67 percent of the wealthy watched less than one hour of TV per day, while 77 percent of the poor watched more than one hour per day. Thinking back on it now, that's how my dad got me those first few jobs by simply meeting total strangers and talking to them. I also remember Hal Gruskin telling me "If you don't ask, the answer is an automatic no".

The nice thing about being so young is that you can ask "dumb" questions which adults are many times too embarrassed to ask. Now is the time to ask as many questions as you can think of without fear of embarrassment. One question you might think about asking adults is "Have you ever read a book about ways to accumulate wealth?" You might be surprised at the number of "No's" you get and how many people don't know how the financial world works.

You need the experience of walking into a bank and opening an account yourself, *providing your old enough and have a Social Security number*. If you don't have one yet, call the Social Security Administration office near you and find out how to get one, there is no age limitation. Don't wait for Mom to do it for you.

Good luck and let the journey begin! YOU CAN MAKE IT HAPPEN!

> "Change almost never fails because it's too early. It almost always fails because it's too late." Seth Godin

SCHEDULING TIME

In a review of Why Time Flies: A Mostly Scientific Investigation, <u>The Economist</u> opined, "Time is such a slippery thing. It ticks away, neutrally, yet it also flies and collapses, and is more often lost than found. Days can feel eternal but a month can gallop past. So, is time ever perceived objectively? Is this experience innate or is it learned? And how long is now, anyway?" Such questions have puzzled philosophers and scientists for over 2,000 years.

> "How did it get so late so soon?" --Dr. Seuss, American author

My theory is this: When you are one year old, one day represents one 365th of your life and seems like a long time. When you're thirteen years old, one day is one 4,745[th] of your life, a much smaller fraction. Even so, fifth grade seemed dreadfully forever to me. When you're my age, one day represents one 24,455[th] of my life, an even smaller fraction, and it seems to buzz by very fast. I believe your brain compares each day's time to all previous time you've lived and therefore feels like it's going by faster as you age. I've got to plan my days in order to get things accomplished. Then again as Tony Robbins said, "If it isn't scheduled, it's not going to happen".

Here's a thought to ponder: Everyone has the same number of hours per day and yet, being independent, we all devote our time to things that we *want* to devote our time to. We all become a product of what we think and what we devote our time to. When people say things like, "I don't have time to (fill in the blank with: study, work, teach my kids to read or whatever) they are really stating their priorities (devotion) is to something else. Yet, today, every person old enough to hold an iPhone or iPad has time to keep their nose buried in the screen image. Now of course, there is a time for work and for play. There is a time to devote (invest in) to your young children as they grow up on a daily basis, not just on some exotic vacation every six months.

The point is you have choices to make with your time and how it is spent. Every day is a learning day no matter what age you are. You learn most things out of the classroom and in the field (real life) anyway. You certainly need a basic education that will prepare you for the next steps in life, be it going to college or learning a trade, but learning is not something you're going to do for a certain number of years and then quit. You will be learning something everyday for the rest of your life. Everyone wants a sense of accomplishment and if you set goals and schedule your time properly you will develop a remarkable feeling, a sense like having successfully climbed Mount Everest. If you play a particular video game often enough, you may be able to achieve level 14 in World of WarCraft or whatever. This, I believe, is a *false* sense of accomplishment and although you played the game better than anyone in the neighborhood, you have to ask yourself what did it get me? It actually proved that you have the ability to do anything you set your mind to. What's that going to be worth five years from now?

Some people have said to "Live for the now" and don't worry about the future. Others are more correct when they say "It's hard to hit a target if you don't aim just a little".

John Wooden said success is built block by block when it comes to building your "pyramid of success". He also said success is an equal opportunity player in regard to family, career or any other endeavors.

"You miss 100% of the shots you don't take" Wayne Gretzky

"You were born to win, but to be a winner, you must plan to win, prepare to win, and expect to win." ZIG ZIGLAR

"The true sign of intelligence is not knowledge, but imagination." Albert Einstein

Now, good luck, and be persistent!

REFERENCES AND RECOMMENDED READING

A COLLECTION of THOUGHTS ON LIFE, Dale Brown, coach

GETTING OVER THE FOUR HURDLES OF LIFE, Coach Dale Brown

HOW TO GET RICH, Felix Dennis, founder of Maxim Magazine

SHARING THE WEALTH, Alex Spanos, owner of San Diego Charges

REAL ESTATE, The World's Greatest Wealth Builder, Carleton Sheets

REAL ESTATE INVESTING FOR DUMMIES, Eric Tyson MBA and Robert Griswold MSBA

Rich Dads Advisors, REAL ESTATE RICHES, Dolf De Roos PHD

MONEY: MASTER OF THE GAME (or any book written by) Tony Robbins

UNSHAKEABLE Tony Robbins

THE ENABLER, Angelyn Miller

THE SECRET OF HAPPINESS, Billy Graham

I LOVE CAPITALISM, Ken Langone, co-founder of Home Depot

THE STRANGEST SECRET, Earl Nightingale

THE GAMBLER, The Kirk Kerkorian Story, by William Rempel

WHAT I LEARNED LOSING A MILLION DOLLARS, by Jim Paul and Brendan Moynihan

COMPLETE IDIOT'S GUIDE TO PERSONAL FINANCE, by Sarah Young Fisher and Susan Shelly

THE ART OF THE DEAL, Donald Trump with Charles Leerhsen

THE SPIRIT TO SERVE, J. W. Marriott

NEVER STOP DREAMING, Carl Karcher

POUR YOUR HEART INTO IT, Howard Schultz

THE LUCK FACTOR, Dr. Richard Wiseman

LUCKY YOU, Proven Strategies For Finding Good Fortune, Randall Fitzgerald

RICH DAD POOR DAD, Robert T. Kiyosaki, (or any book by Robert Kiyosaki)

GRINDING IT OUT, by Ray Kroc with Robert Anderson

FAMILY FORTUNES, by Bill Bonner and Will Bonner

PYRAMID OF SUCCESS, by John Wooden

BITCOIN PIZZA, by Samantha Radocchia

MONDAY MORNING LEADERSHIP, by David Cotrell

TUESDAYS WITH MORRIE, by Mitch Albom

WHAT ON EARTH AM I HERE FOR, Rick Warren

ROBERT'S RULES OF ORDER, Newly Revised, Henry M. Robert II

A CURIOUS MIND, Secret to a Bigger Life, Brian Grazer

THE FORMULA = The Universal Laws of Success, Albert-Laszlo Barabasi

UNSTOPPABLE PROSPERITY, Charles Payne, Professional Investor

WARREN BUFFETT and the INTERPRETATION OF FINANCIAL STATEMENTS, by Mary Buffett

THE LAZY WAY TO INVEST IN REAL ESTATE, Robert Kiyosaki